THE HA

MW01017074

For my dear friend
Chris Hardy

FREEDOM UNDER THE LAW on law

on his visit + the law

21ˢᵗ May 1994

Tom Denning

and 95¼

AUSTRALIA
The Law Book Company Ltd.
Sydney : Melbourne : Brisbane

CANADA AND U.S.A.
The Carswell Company Ltd.
Toronto

INDIA
N. M. Tripathi Private Ltd.
Bombay

ISRAEL
Steimatzky's Agency Ltd.
Jerusalem : Tel Aviv : Haifa

NEW ZEALAND
Sweet & Maxwell (N.Z.) Ltd.
Wellington

PAKISTAN
Pakistan Law House
Karachi

FREEDOM
UNDER THE LAW

BY

THE RIGHT HONOURABLE

SIR ALFRED DENNING

*One of the Lords Justices of His Majesty's Court of Appeal
in England*

LONDON

STEVENS & SONS LIMITED

1949

First Edition	-	-	-	-	-	1949
Second Impression		-	-	-		1949
Third Impression -		-	-	-		1950
Fourth Impression -		-	-	-		1950
Fifth Impression -		-	-	-		1952
Sixth Impression (reset)			-	-		1954
Seventh Impression		-	-	-		1962
Eighth Impression -		-	-	-		1968
Ninth Impression -		-	-	-		1971
Tenth Impression		-	-	-		1974
Eleventh Impression	-		-	-		1977
Twelfth Impression		-	-	-		1979
Thirteenth Impression -			-	-		1986

Published by
Stevens & Sons Limited
of 11 New Fetter Lane
in the City of London
and printed by Page
Bros (Norwich) Ltd

ISBN 0 420 42140 8.

CONTENTS

THE HAMLYN TRUST

THE Hamlyn Trust came into existence under the will of the late Miss Emma Warburton Hamlyn of Torquay, who died in 1941 aged 80. She came of an old and well-known Devon family. Her father, William Russell Hamlyn, practised in Torquay as a solicitor for many years. She was a woman of dominant character, intelligent and cultured, well versed in literature, music, and art, and a ·lover of her country. She inherited a taste for law, and studied the subject. She travelled frequently on the Continent and about the Mediterranean and gathered impressions of comparative jurisprudence and ethnology.

Miss Hamlyn bequeathed the residue of her estate in terms which were thought vague. The matter was taken to the Chancery division of the High Court, which on November 29, 1948, approved a Scheme for the administration of the Trust. Paragraph 3 of the Scheme is as follows :—

' The object of this charity is the furtherance by lectures or otherwise among the Common People of the United Kingdom of Great Britain and Northern Ireland of the knowledge of the Comparative Jurisprudence and the Ethnology of the Chief European Countries, including the United Kingdom, and the circumstances of the growth of such Jurisprudence to the intent that the Common People of the United Kingdom may realise the privileges which in law and custom they enjoy in comparison with other European Peoples and realising and appreciating such privileges may recognise the responsibilities and obligations attaching to them.'

The Trustees under the Scheme number nine, viz. :

(*a*) Sir EDMUND BALL,   ⎫ Executors of
Mr. S. K. COLERIDGE,   ⎬ Miss Hamlyn's
Mr. J. R. WARBURTON   ⎭   Will.

(*b*) Representatives of the Universities of London, Wales, Leeds, Glasgow and Belfast, viz :

Professor G. W. KEETON,
Professor D. L. Ll. DAVIES,
Professor B. A. WORTLEY,
Professor D. S. MACLAGAN,
and Belfast, vacant.

(*c*) The Principal of the University College of the South-West, *ex-officio*.

The Trustees decided to organise courses of lectures of high interest and quality by persons of eminence under the auspices of co-operating Universities with a view to the lectures being made available in book form to a wide public.

This first series of four lectures was given by the Rt. Hon. Lord Justice Denning in the Senate House, London University, in October and November, 1949.

JOHN MURRAY,

November, 1949.   *Chairman of the Trustees.*

PERSONAL FREEDOM

PERSONAL FREEDOM

I HOPE you have not come expecting a scholarly discourse replete with copious references. If you have, I fear you will be disappointed : for, I have come as the Hamlyn Trust bids me, to speak, as it were, to the common people of England and to further amongst them the knowledge of their laws, so that they may realise their privileges and likewise their responsibilities. So if I refer to matters which you know full well, I hope you will forgive me. Not that it is any discredit to any of us to be one of the common people of England. It is indeed the greatest privilege that any man can have : for the common people of England have succeeded to the greatest heritage of all—the heritage of freedom : and it is that which I have come to talk about—freedom under the law.

Let me start with an instance of how the courts approach the subject. Whenever one of the King's judges takes his seat, there is one application which by long tradition has priority over all others. Counsel has but to say ' My Lord, I have an application which concerns the liberty of the subject ' and forthwith the judge will put all other matters aside and hear it. It may be an application for a writ of habeas corpus, or an application for bail, but, whatever form it takes, it is heard first. This is of course only a matter of procedure, but the English law respecting the freedom of the individual has been built up from the procedure of the courts : and this simple instance of priority in point of time contains within it the fundamental principle that, where there is any conflict between the freedom of the individual and any other rights or interests, then no matter how great or powerful those others may be, the freedom of the humblest citizen shall prevail over it.

These are fine sentiments which you will find expressed in the laws of other countries too ; but rights are no good unless you can enforce them ; and it is in their enforcement that English law has shown its peculiar genius. The task is one of getting the right balance. The freedom of the individual, which is so dear to us, has to be balanced with his duty ; for, to be sure every one owes a duty to the society of which he forms part. The balance has changed remarkably during the last 100 years. Previously the freedom of the individual carried with it a freedom to acquire and use his property as he wished, a freedom to contract and so forth : but these freedoms were so much abused that in our time they have been counterbalanced by the duty to use one's property and powers for the good of society as a whole. In some foreign countries this duty has been carried to such a pitch that freedom, as we know it, no longer exists. If the people of those countries choose to put up with such a system that is their affair. All that needs to be said about it is that it is not the English view of human society. What matters in England is that each man should be free to develop his own personality to the full : and the only duties which should restrict this freedom are those which are necessary to enable everyone else to do the same. Whenever these interests are nicely balanced, the scale goes down on the side of freedom. In these lectures I hope to show how the English law has kept in the past the balance between individual freedom and social duty : and how it should keep the balance in the social revolution of today, drawing on the experience and laws of other European countries for the lessons we can learn from them.

PERSONAL FREEDOM

Let me first define my terms. By personal freedom I mean the freedom of every law-abiding citizen to think what he will, to say what he will, and to go where he will on his lawful occasions without let or hindrance from any other persons. Despite all the great changes that have come about in the other freedoms, this freedom has in our country remained intact. It must be matched, of course, with social security, by which I mean the peace and good order of the community in which we live. The freedom of the just man is worth little to him if he can be preyed upon by the murderer or thief. Every society must have the means to protect itself from marauders. It must have powers to arrest, to search, and to imprison those who break the laws. So long as those powers are properly exercised, they are themselves the safeguards of freedom. But powers may be abused, and, if those powers are abused, there is no tyranny like them. It leads to a state of affairs when the police may arrest any man and throw him into prison without cause assigned. It leads to the search of his home and belongings on the slightest pretext—or on none. It leads to the hated gestapo and the police State. It leads to extorted confessions and to trials which are a mockery of justice. The moral of it all is that a true balance must be kept between personal freedom on the one hand and social security on the other. It has been done here, and is being done. But how ?

HABEAS CORPUS

In the first place the law says that no man is to be imprisoned except by judgment of the King's Courts or whilst awaiting trial by them. This freedom is safeguarded by the most famous writ in England, the writ of Habeas Corpus. Whenever any man in England is detained against his will, not by sentence of the King's Courts, but by anyone else, then he or anyone on his behalf is entitled to apply to any of the judges of the High Court to determine whether his detention is lawful or not. The court will then, by this writ, command the gaoler or whoever is detaining him, to bring him before the court ; and, unless the detention is shown to be lawful, the court will at once set him free.

This was not always so. In 1627, when the executive Government cast Sir Thomas Darnel and four other knights into prison because they would not subscribe money for the King, the Court of

King's Bench, to its disgrace, held that if a man were committed by command of the King he was not to be delivered by habeas corpus.[1] Those were the evil days when the judges took their orders from the executive. But the people of England overthrew the Government which so assailed their liberties, and passed statutes which gave the writ its present power. Never thereafter have the judges taken their orders from anyone.

So in 1771, when the coloured slave James Sommersett was held in irons on board a ship lying in the Thames and bound for Jamaica, Lord Mansfield declared his detention to be unlawful. ' The air of England is too pure for any slave to breathe,' he said, ' Let the black go free,' and the slave went free.[2] And take a modern instance, in 1949 when the communist Gerhardt Eisler was taken forcibly from a Polish ship in Cowes Roads, Sir Laurence Dunne held that there was no lawful ground on which he could be handed over to the United States.[3] It was a case of ' let the " red " go free.' The law of England knows no colour bar, whether it be the colour of a man's skin or of his politics.

Nor are the King's Courts to be overawed by high officers of the State. So in 1947 when the Army authorities took a bank clerk from his home in Lancashire, in the middle of the night, carried him off to Germany and court-martialled him there, the

---

[1] *Darnel's Case*, 3 St.Tr. 1.

[2] *R. v. Sommersett*, 20 St.Tr. 1.

[3] This was a case of refusal to extradite. If Eisler had still been detained, a writ of habeas corpus would no doubt have issued.

Lord Chief Justice of England called on the Secretary
of State for War to justify his conduct by law ; and
when he failed to do so, directed that a writ of
habeas corpus should issue.   The bank clerk left the
court a free man.[4]   It was thus shown again in our
time, as it has often been shown before in our long
history, that the executive Government has no right
to deprive any man of his freedom except by due course
of law.   The Attorney-General of the day seems to
have thought that the decision was wrong but there
was nothing he could do to alter it.   Once a man
is set free under a writ of habeas corpus, there is
no appeal open to those who would imprison him.[5]

Moreover if the first court to which he applies
refuses to grant the writ of habeas corpus, he can
apply to any other High Court judge and ask him to
hear the case afresh : and if he can persuade but one
judge that he is unlawfully detained, he will be set
free.   This is an accident of procedure,[5] as are many
other incidents of the writ, but these accidents are all
on the side of freedom.

This writ of habeas corpus is available, not only
where the original detention is unlawful, but also
when a man, who has been lawfully arrested on a
criminal charge, is kept in prison without trial.   The
police have no right to hold him on their own
authority for more than a day.   He must be brought
before a magistrate within 24 hours and it is then for

[4] R. v. *Governor of Wandsworth Prison, ex p. Boydell* [1948] 2 K.B. 193.
[5] A note on Habeas Corpus, by Lord Goddard, 65 L.Q.R. 30.   So
also whenever a man is found not guilty of an offence with which
he is charged, there is no appeal open to the prosecution who think
him guilty.

the magistrate to decide whether he shall be further
detained pending trial or let out on bail.   If the
magistrate refuses to let him out on bail, the man can
apply to a High Court judge for bail.   No person in
this country who is committed to prison on a charge
of crime can be kept long in confinement because he
can insist upon either being let out on bail or else of
being brought to speedy trial.

All this is of course familiar law but I make no
apology for saying it again now, because I wish to
point the contrast between this effective procedure
and the procedure of other countries.   The freedom-
loving countries of Western Europe have the same
principles as we have—there, as here, no one must
be imprisoned except by due course of law—but
they have not the same procedure for enforcing these
principles.   They have no procedure corresponding
to our writ of habeas corpus.   They have no means
whereby a man who is unlawfully detained can be at
once set free.   All that a man can do there is to lodge
a complaint with a police officer, who ought then to
transmit it to a magistrate : but if the police officer
does not do his duty, as for instance if he refuses or
neglects to put it before a magistrate, the man has
no remedy except to charge the police officer with
an offence.[6]   There is no machinery by means of
which he can, so to speak, pass by the officials and go
straight to the judge : nor is there any means of
obtaining a speedy trial.   This was pointedly shown
in 1946 when a British soldier was arrested in

---

[6] Faustin Hélie, *Practique Criminelle*, 15th ed., p. 49, commenting
on Art. 117 of the Code.

Belgium and charged with having committed a
murder there.   The preliminary investigations took
so long that more than a year passed before he was
brought to trial : and he was kept in custody all the
time.   The delay seemed by our standards to be a
denial of justice.   Questions were asked in Parliament
and representations were made by our Government
to the Belgian Government.   He was eventually
tried and acquitted.   In this country he would not
have been detained for so long without trial.   If he
had not been brought before the next Assizes he would
have had a right to be let out on bail—a right which
he could enforce by writ of habeas corpus.

Detaining the ' Fifth Column '

So much therefore for the principle that no man
is to be imprisoned except by judgment of the King's
Courts : but come now to the exception from it,
for the exception has more lessons to teach us today
than the principle itself.   The exception arose from
the need to detain fifth columnists in time of war.
In time of peace, of course, a man can only be sent to
prison for crimes which he has committed in the
past.   He cannot be detained by the executive simply
because they think he may commit crimes in the
future.   But in time of war this rule has to be
abrogated.   If there are traitors in our midst, we
cannot afford to wait until we catch them in the act
of blowing up our bridges or giving our military
secrets to the enemy.   We cannot run the risk of
leaving them at large.   We must detain them on

suspicion. In the recent war, therefore, by Regulation 18B, the Secretary of State was given power to detain a man if he had reasonable cause to believe that he was of hostile origin or of hostile associations and that by reason thereof it was necessary to exercise control over him.

This power to imprison a man without trial, not for what he had already done, but for what he might hereafter do, was entrusted by Parliament to the executive. It could not be reviewed by the ordinary Courts of law. Lord Atkin, in a great judgment, vigorously dissented from this view. He declared that : ' In this country, amid the clash of arms, the laws are not silent. They may be changed, but they speak the same language in war as in peace. It has always been one of the pillars of freedom, one of the principles of liberty for which we are now fighting, that the judges are no respecters of persons and stand between the subject and any attempted encroachments on his liberty by the executive, alert to see that any coercive action is justified in law. In this case I have listened to arguments which might have been addressed acceptably to the Court of King's Bench in the time of Charles I. I protest, even if I do it alone, against a strained construction put on words with the effect of giving an uncontrolled power of imprisonment to the minister '.[7] Lord Atkin's view did not prevail, because the other Law Lords took a different view of the needs of the country in time of war. But Lord Atkin's dissent will have served a useful purpose if it reminds us that this

[7] *Liversidge* v. *Sir John Anderson* [1942] A.C. at p. 244.

war-time exception must not be allowed to be introduced into this country in time of peace, or at all events only in the gravest emergency. If proof of this were needed it can be found by comparing our war-time procedure with the procedure in the Soviet Union today.

Our procedure can best be shown by taking a concrete case. A clergyman of the Church of England had before the war been invited by the Nazi authorities to visit Germany at their expense. He was shown the best side of the National Socialist system and was greatly impressed with it. This was, of course, known in his parish and, after the war broke out, his church was boycotted. He became known as the 'Nazi parson'. Then, when there was imminent danger of invasion, the population was alarmed. The police collected information about him and put it before the officers who were charged with investigation of 'fifth column' activities—called M.I.5. The clergyman was taken before a lawyer, who questioned him closely, but he had no solicitor himself. Legal representation was not allowed to him. The clergyman stated that he thought National-Socialism was excellent for Germany but that he did not think it would answer in this country : and he protested that he would not do anything to help the Germans. It was clear that his attitude was solely due to his own conscience. The question was, of course, whether his enthusiasm for National-Socialism was so great that he might, for instance, give refuge to a German parachutist who came by night to his vicarage—which was in a lonely

village in the country. It was decided that, with the
threat of invasion so near, no risks could be taken.
So he was detained. This meant that he was kept in
a prison for some time, then in various detention
camps, and it was nearly three years before he was
released. Yet he had done nothing wrong.

PROCEDURE IN SOVIET RUSSIA

Now try to put yourself in the place of a
communist in Soviet Russia today. Start off, if you
can, with the proposition that the communist way of
life is the best way of life : that all goods should be
held in common and that no one should have any
advantage in property or wealth over anyone else ;
and that the duty of each is to devote himself to the
welfare of everyone else. Then it is easy to persuade
yourself that this way of life is so important that it
must be safeguarded against anything which may
endanger it. If you feel that there are insidious
enemies in and around you who are concerned to
destroy this way of life, you will soon come to regard
yourself as engaged in a holy war in defence of
communism : and at that point you will have a
setting in which you can justify the detention of
suspects hostile to your cause on the same grounds
as we detained suspects in the recent war. Whereas
the safety of our country was imperilled, it is the
communist way of life which, in their view, is
imperilled. Whereas there was then a ' hot ' war,
in their view there is now a cold war. Thence it is
only a logical step to say that you cannot wait till the
steed is stolen before you shut the stable door. The

safety of the community demands that a suspect shall be detained before he commits sabotage. That is the principle on which the Soviet jurists justify their procedure ; and it is at bottom the same principle as we invoked during the war.

Article 7 of their Code bears a striking similarity to our Regulation 18B. It authorises the detention of persons ' who are a danger either by reason of their dangerous associations or by reason of their previous activities '. Our Regulation 18B authorises the detention of persons believed to be ' of hostile associations or to have been recently concerned in acts prejudicial to the public safety '.

You can understand their point of view best by looking at the position in reverse. It would be quite easy here, would it not, to find reasons for interning all communists and fellow-travellers. It could be said with force that they are such an insidious danger to our way of life that we cannot risk leaving them at large. We have not, however, gone so far as that. We have not deprived them of their liberty but only of access to military secrets. Whether it will in time become necessary to fight them with their own weapons I do not know : but I sincerely hope not. Freedom must be true to itself or it will perish. This is a war of ideologies, which is not to be won by throwing people behind bars, but by ' having your loins girt about with truth '.

Thus you see that the exception which we introduced in war-time has become in Russia a peace-time principle. It shows the difference in our way of life. In the English way of life the freedom of the individual must not be impaired except so far as absolutely necessary. In the totalitarian way of life the freedom of the individual must always give way to the interests of the State. Concede, if you wish, that, as an ideology, communism has much to be said for it : nevertheless the danger in a totalitarian system is that those in control of the State will, sooner or later, come to identify their own interests, or the interests of their own party, with those of the State : and when that happens the freedom of the individual has to give way to the interests of the persons in power. We have had all that out time and again in our long history : and we know the answer. It is that the executive government must never be allowed more power than is absolutely necessary. They must always be made subject to the law ; and there must be judges in the land who are ' no respecters of persons and stand between the subject and any encroachment on his liberty by the executive '. We taught the kings that from Runnymede to the scaffold at Whitehall : and we have not had any serious trouble about it since. But we cannot afford, in these days, to be off our guard. The modern way of life in all countries involves more and more power being entrusted to the executive. Total war demands it. So does the socialised State. Look abroad and see what happened in Nazi Germany and happens today in Soviet Russia and in the satellite countries such as Hungary. The judges take their orders from the party in power : and so there is no one to stand between the subject and the executive.

The war-time power to detain suspects represents the high-water mark of power of the executive of this country. Looking back it can safely be said that the power was not abused. The reason was that it was administered by men who could be trusted not to allow any man's liberty to be taken away without good cause. The legal advisers who advised the Regional Commissioners, and the Chairmen of Committees who advised the Home Secretary, were, most of them, King's Counsel who gave their services without reward and who, by all their experience, training, and tradition, could be trusted not lightly to interfere with any man's freedom. Indeed, many of them now hold high judicial office. Finally there was a conscientious and careful Home Secretary who was answerable to a Parliament which was ever vigilant in defence of liberty.

Freedom from Arbitrary Arrest

Now let me leave the first principle by which our personal freedom is protected, and the exception to it ; and come to the second principle, which is that no man shall be arrested except for reasonable cause allowed by law. This principle is of course the same as the first but it deals with a specific aspect of it, namely, the power of arrest for a criminal offence. It is safeguarded by requiring every person who makes an arrest, whether he be a policeman or private individual, to justify the arrest, if called upon, in a court of law. A policeman in this country is not allowed to arrest a man simply because he in good faith suspects him of a criminal offence, but only if he on reasonable grounds suspects him : and his grounds can be examined in the courts. This state of the law has only been reached by degrees : and the story of it is the story of the police in England— a story of which we have every reason to be proud.[8]

We had no professional police in England until comparatively recent times. By the common law it was the duty of every man, not only to keep the peace himself, but also to arrest, or help to arrest, anyone who had committed a felony. On a cry of ' Stop Thief ' all had to cease work and join in the pursuit of the offender. There were, of course, parish constables and night watchmen who had to levy the hue and cry and follow ' with all the town ', but these were a standing joke for years. You will remember how Shakespeare poked fun at them : Constable Dogberry's instruction to watchmen is 'You shall make no noise in the streets : for, for the watch to babble and talk is most tolerable and not to be endured '. To which the watchmen reply ' We will rather sleep than talk : we know what belongs to a watch '. In the eighteenth century the watchmen still kept up their reputation for somnolence. Lee, in his *History of Police in England*, describes how ' it was a popular amusement amongst young men of the town to imprison watchmen by upsetting their watchboxes on top of them as they dozed within ; and the young blood who could exhibit to his friends a collection of trophies such as lanterns, staves or rattles was much

---

[8] See ' Legal and Social Aspects of Arrest ' by Jerome Hall, 49 H.L.R. 566.

accounted of in smart society. The newspapers were never tired of skits at the parochial watch '.[9]

It was in 1753 that the first step was taken towards professional police. There was at that time an acute ' crime wave '. So Henry Fielding presented a plan to the Duke of Newcastle as a result of which they organised the Bow Street Runners. These were men specially quick in catching thieves. They were paid from private funds. In 1805 John Fielding organised the horse patrol to guard the roads. These proved very effective and there was a sharp fall in the number of crimes of violence. But it was still a lay organisation. In 1829, however, Sir Robert Peel brought into being the modern disciplined efficient force. It was regarded by many as a threat to freedom. Anonymous placards were broadcast reading ' Liberty or death ! Englishmen ! Britons ! ! and Honest Men ! ! ! The time has at length arrived. All London meets on Tuesday. Come armed. We assure you from ocular demonstration that 6,000 cutlasses have been removed from the Tower for the use of Peel's bloody gang. These damned police are now to be armed. Englishmen will you put up with this ? '.[10] There was clearly a need to balance conflicting interests. It has been done. But how ?

POWER OF ARREST

The conflict has been solved by the judges, who have granted to the police very few privileges—

[9] Lee, *History of Police in England*, 184-5.
[10] Lee, p. 251.

indeed, only such privileges as are absolutely essential for them to do their work, and have in all other respects treated them as subject to the same rules as any private citizen. Take the power of arrest. Until the eighteenth century a constable—there were, of course, only the parish constables in those days— had no greater power of arrest than any private individual. He had not only to have reasonable suspicion of the man, but he had to prove that the crime—the felony—had actually been committed.[11] This gave a constable a grand excuse for doing nothing: because when a householder came up to him and complained that his goods had been stolen and pointed out the thief, the constable could say ' How do I know your goods have been stolen ? ' The constable could justly say that he was in a difficulty : for if a private citizen made a reasonable charge of felony against another, the constable was bound by his oath of office to arrest the accused man, but nevertheless the constable was not protected by the law if it should turn out that the informant was mistaken.[12] No wonder that Dogberry advised his watchmen not to meddle with a thief. When they asked ' If we know him to be a thief, shall we not lay hands on him ? ' Dogberry replied ' Truly by your office you may : but the most peaceable way for you, if you do take a thief, is to let him show himself what he is and steal out of your company '.

The unsatisfactory state of the law was modified

[11] 2 Hale, *P.C.* 91-2.
[12] See *per* Lord du Parcq in *Christie* v. *Leachinsky* [1947] A.C. at pp. 596-7.

by the judges. The pressure of events indeed made it imperative. The industrial revolution had, indeed, increased the need for security, protection and order. And the turbulent state of the country is shown by the Gordon Riots, in which the rioters not only stormed Newgate Prison and released the inmates but they also burnt the houses of the judges, including the house of Lord Mansfield. It was clearly necessary to strengthen the powers of the constables. Accordingly, in that very year, 1780, Lord Mansfield laid it down that if a private citizen made a charge of felony, that was sufficient justification for a constable, and his assistants, to arrest the person accused, although no felony had, in fact, been committed.[13] It was held that they could act on bare information without doing anything to verify it.[14]

For a time it was even thought unnecessary for the constable to inquire into the reasonableness of the charge but it became obvious that, if a constable were allowed to arrest individuals on unreasonable charges, freedom would be greatly imperilled. The balance had swung too far against individual freedom. The judges therefore restored the balance. In 1827 it was laid down that even a constable is not allowed to make an arrest unless he has reasonable ground for believing that the accused has committed a felony.[15] The necessary adjustments in the law were thus achieved just in time for the coming of professional police two years later. The increased need for social

[13] *Samuel v. Payne*, 1 Doug. 359.
[14] See the law stated by Buller J. quoted in [1947] A.C. at p. 597.
[15] *Beckwith v. Philby* (1827) 6 B. & C. 635.

security was met by giving the police just so much extra power of arrest as was necessary and no more.

Since that time Parliament has extended the power of arrest so as to include many misdemeanours as well as felonies but the underlying principle has remained untouched. No greater power must be given than is absolutely necessary for the protection of life and property. In all cases Parliament has insisted that an officer shall only arrest a man if he has reasonable ground for believing that he has committed the offence in question : and if the reasonableness of his action is afterwards called into question, it is for the judges to determine it.[16] The working of the law was well shown a few years ago when some customs officers boarded a steamship which had arrived at Liverpool and found a box of cigars concealed under the mattress of a bunk in an unoccupied state room. It turned out that the cigars belonged to a ship's steward who had not declared them. So the officers arrested him. The steward was acquitted by the magistrate because there was a real doubt in the case : but the arrest was held by the House of Lords to be justifiable. Lord Simon pointed out that ' if officers of customs cannot detain a man who is coming off a ship whom they suspect on reasonable grounds of endeavouring to defraud the customs . . . the working of our customs laws is likely to be seriously impeded '.[17]

[16] See the instances given by Lord Atkin in *Liversidge* v. *Anderson* [1942] A.C. at p. 229.
[17] *Barnard* v. *Gorman* [1941] A.C. 378.

POLICE POWERS

The judges have been careful never to allow the police to overstep the mark. Quite recently a sergeant of the Liverpool police took a rag-and-bone man into custody because he thought he was a receiver of stolen goods : but he did not tell him that that was the reason why he arrested him. It was held that the sergeant's act was unlawful, because every citizen is entitled to know on what charge he is seized. No policeman is entitled to go up to a man and say ' Come along with me ' without giving his reasons, unless the reason is obvious. Lord Simonds spoke in the tradition of centuries when he said ' Blind unquestioning obedience is the law of tyrants and of slaves : it does not yet flourish on English soil. . . . Arrested with or without a warrant, the subject is entitled to know why he is deprived of his freedom, if only in order that he may, without a moment's delay, take such steps as will enable him to regain it.'[18]

If the police should overstep the mark and arrest a man when they have no lawful authority to do so, he has the same rights as against the police as he would have against any private individual who unlawfully arrested him. He is entitled to resist the unlawful arrest, if need be, by force. If a ticket collector or a policeman tried to arrest a passenger for travelling without paying his fare, when he was willing to give his name and address, he would be entitled to knock them down rather than go with them. If he submitted to the arrest and went, he would be entitled to obtain

---

[18] *Christie* v. *Leachinsky* [1947] A.C. 573.

his immediate release by means of a writ of habeas corpus : and, after obtaining his release, he would be entitled to bring an action for damages against them for false imprisonment.

It should not be supposed that, in laying down these principles, the judges have any desire to encourage citizens to resist lawful authority. They do not. Nor has that been their effect. It is simply a question of balancing the conflicting interests. Social security requires that the police should have power to make a lawful arrest, but individual freedom requires that a man should have power to resist an unlawful arrest and, if need be, by force. That is proved by the experience of France. In that country no citizen has any right to defend himself against the police or other public officers. Even if they are acting quite unlawfully, as, for instance, if they arrest a man without any justification at all, or beat him quite unmercifully ; or if they force an entry into his house by night without any warrant, he must submit to it all. He must not hit back and must not defend himself or his house. If he does he is guilty of the criminal offence of rebellion.[19] The only thing a citizen can do is to submit and complain afterwards. We are told by a writer on French Criminal Procedure that this led to ' the " passage à tabac ", which took its name from the passage which leads from the charge-room to the cells in any police station. If a prisoner had violently resisted arrest, that passage, which was usually dark, was lined on both sides by policemen, who rained blows on the unfortunate

[19] Panstin Hélie (see note 6), p. 161.

accused as he passed between them to the cell. This cowardly practice was not even officially denied, but efforts have been made to suppress it, and probably now only occurs in exceptional cases '.[20]   This shows how, even in a free country, the law, by giving to police officers an authority which is wider than absolutely necessary, may lead to grave abuse.

THE BALANCING OF INTERESTS

The way in which we in England have balanced conflicting interests on this important point—the power of arrest—is a model.   The police are not regarded here as the strong arm of the executive, but as the friends of the people.   So much is this the case that any case of assaulting or obstructing the police arouses great indignation.   And no one is inclined to resist the authority of the police, because it can safely be assumed to be lawfully used.   The reason is twofold : on the one hand, the law does not put into the hands of the police any more power than is absolutely necessary : on the other hand, the police are, on the whole, such a fine body of men that they do not abuse the powers which they have.

Ever since the professional police have been formed the greatest care has been used to select the right type of man—young men of excellent character, from good homes, usually of sturdy country stock, who, without knowing it, have born in them a sense of fair play and calmness in emergency, and, withal, a respect for law and order.   And they have been well

[20] Wright on French Criminal Procedure, 44 L.Q.R. at p. 339.

trained and well led. If you reflect on the hostile mood of the people when a police force was first introduced and consider the confidence which we all have in them now, you will realise how great a work has been accomplished. The Home Secretary put it very well a little time ago : ' There is a great distinction between the British police force and the police of other countries. The British policeman is a civilian discharging civilian duties and merely put into uniform so that those who need his help know exactly where to look for assistance '.

We must not, however, be too complacent about this. We must always be vigilant to see that there is no deterioration in the standards of the police. This can be shown by two instances. A junior barrister was once engaged to prosecute a man for loitering on railway premises with intent to commit a felony. He had been found in a compartment in a carriage in a siding. This man's case was that he had only gone there to sleep. To prove that this was his purpose he asked the railway policeman who found him ' Had I got my boots off ? ' The policeman said ' Yes ' and the man was acquitted. But a metropolitan detective said to the barrister afterwards, with a significant look, ' If I had found him he wouldn't have had his boots off '. His desire to get a conviction of a man whom he believed to be guilty would have led him to perjure himself. Again, when a special constable was allotted a beat on the main road, a regular police-man said to him, pointedly, ' A main road beat—that should be worth 10s. anyhow '. He was apparently prepared to overlook offences in return for a money

B

payment. And cases do occasionally come before the courts in which policemen have proved unworthy of the trust imposed in them. Fortunately these cases are rare. But they show that a proper balance cannot be kept unless the police is manned by men of the highest integrity. It is just as important that the police should be honest and fair in all their dealings as that judges should be.

Freedom from Oppression

Let me come now to a matter which is closely allied to the freedom from arbitrary arrest, and that is the freedom from oppression whilst under arrest. The history of the world shows many instances of oppression, usually for the sake of getting people to confess their guilt or to implicate others. Torture was used in the older civilisation of Athens and Rhodes and even in the Roman Empire : but the most enlightened jurists—Cicero for example—gave their unequivocal testimony against it. Brutality is not used today but some other means not known to us is used. Takes the cases of Cardinal Mindzenty and Mr. Rajk. Those men actually made full confessions in open court with all appearance of telling the truth. Yet most people outside the countries concerned think that they have been induced by some means or other to say what is untrue. ' The most credible theory ' says *The Times* ' is that Soviet psychologists have perfected methods of mental aggression which can be applied with success to a great variety of victims . . . the same method, with suitable variation in approach, might be applied to a Communist Cabinet Minister and a Catholic Cardinal '.[21]

TORTURE

We are horrified that such methods should be used, and assume that such things could not happen here. But we have only learnt it by a long and painful process. In the reign of Henry VI Sir John Fortescue, Chief Justice of England, declared that ' all tortures and torments of parties accused were directly against the common laws of England '. Such indeed has always been laid down by the judges but, in spite of it, the executive government right down to the year 1640 habitually used to torture prisoners who were accused of treason or other political offences. The object was either to extract a confession which could be used at the trial or to make them disclose who were their confederates.

A celebrated case is that of Felton, who stabbed the Duke of Buckingham in 1628. He confessed to the murder and was called before the King's Council. The *State Trials* give a vivid account of the proceedings.[22] ' The Council much pressed him to confess who set him to do such a bloody act, and if the puritans had no hand therein. He denied that they had. Doctor Laud, Bishop of London, being then at the Council table told him, if he would not confess he would go on the rack. Felton replied if it must be so, he could not tell which of their Lordships

[21] *The Times*, September 26, 1949. See also theory suggested in a letter to the *Daily Telegraph*, October 11, 1949.
[22] 3 *State Trials*, 371.

he might name, for torture might draw unexpected
things from him. . . .   After this he was asked no
more questions but sent back to prison.   The Council
then fell into debate, whether by the law of the land
they could justify putting him to the rack,   The
King, being at the Council, said, " Before any such
thing be done, let the advice of the judges be had
thereon whether it be legal or no " . . . . and on
the 14th November, all the judges being assembled at
Serjeant's Inn, in Fleet Street, agreed in one, that " he
ought not by the law to be tortured by the rack, for
no such punishment is known or allowed by our
law " ".

After this pronouncement by the judges Felton
was not put on the rack, but the executive government still ignored the law.   In 1640 John Archer, a
simple glove-maker, was supposed to have been
concerned in an attack in Archbishop Laud's palace
at Lambeth.   On the 21st May in that year, a warrant
was given under the King's signet, addressed to the
Lieutenant of the Tower, authorising him to cause
John Archer to be carried to the rack, and directing
him, together with the King's Serjeants-at-law Heath
and Whitfield, to examine the prisoner ; and if upon
sight of the rack he should not make a clear answer,
then they were to cause him to be racked as in their
discretion should be thought fit.   This is the last
recorded instance of the infliction of torture in
England.[23]

The common people of England overthrew the
executive   government   which   claimed   such   a

[23] *Jardine on Torture*, p. 109.

monstrous prerogative : and never since has it been known in England. But torture was practised on the continent of Europe right down to the French Revolution. Indeed, shortly before 1793 a man was executed in Paris for the alleged murder of a woman, proved only by his own confession under torture— and the woman was discovered alive two years after the execution of the supposed murderer. In Russia the use of torture in judicial tribunals was first interrupted by a recommendation of the Empress Catherine in 1763 ; and its final abolition as a part of the Russian law was effected by an Imperial Ukase in 1801. Now, after 150 years, a weapon of an unknown kind to extract confessions is used again in Eastern Europe for the same purpose as it was used in times past, namely, the suppression of political opponents of the party in power. If it seems in-conceivable to us here it is because the law of the land does not permit it and the people would not tolerate an executive government which practised it contrary to the law.

Promise of Pardon

After torture was abolished there remained, for a time, another way of obtaining confessions, namely by a promise of a pardon. Evidence obtained by such means is obviously just as unreliable as that obtained by torture. Indeed, in the eighteenth century there was a case of a man who, under promise of pardon, confessed himself guilty with two others, who were tried with him, of the murder of Mr. Harrison at

Campden, in Gloucestershire, but a few years afterwards it appeared that Mr. Harrison was alive. Experiences such as these led the judges, in 1785, to lay down the law that a ' confession forced from the mind by the flattery of hope, or the torture of fear, comes in so questionable a shape that no credit ought to be given to it and therefore it is rejected '.[24] Too great a chastity cannot be preserved upon this subject.[25] This has been the law ever since.

But it is very instructive to note the way in which it has been applied in the case of confessions made to the police. At the time when professional police were introduced there was considerable apprehension about their powers. They were obviously in a position to influence accused men to confess. So the judges made it clear that they would not admit in evidence any confessions which had been in any way improperly obtained by the police. Between 1837 and 1844 there were many cases in which judges ruled that even if a policeman told a prisoner that anything he said might be given in evidence for him, or against him, the subsequent confession was inadmissible.[26] This was obviously carrying the matter too far the other way. But in 1852 the balance was restored. Public apprehension has given way to public confidence in the police, and the prior rulings were overthrown.[27] It was recognised to be right and proper that a policeman should caution a prisoner.

[24] *R. v. Warwickshall* (1783) 1 Leach 263.
[25] *R. v. Thompson* (1783) 1 Leach at p. 293.
[26] *R. v. Drew* (1837) 8 C. & P. 140 ; *R. v. Morton* (1843) 2 M. & R. 514 ; *R. v. Furley* (1844) 1 Cox 76 ; *R. v. Harris* (1844) 1 Cox 106.
[27] *R. v. Baldry* (1852) 2 Den. 430.

Since that time the balance has been kept even. The judges admit in evidence confessions which have been freely and voluntarily made but rigorously exclude any others.

In a case a few years ago at Lincoln Assizes a man was charged with murdering a woman in a house in Scunthorpe. The local police had interviewed him but he said nothing to incriminate himself. Then the officers from Scotland Yard came down and, after very long interviews, obtained a confession from him. The questioning was so prolonged that he was induced to confess by the hope of avoiding further questioning. It was a case of excess of zeal on the part of the officers. At the trial counsel for the prosecution very properly admitted that in the cirumstances it was not a free or voluntary confession : and as there was no other evidence against him, he was acquitted.

So also in a case tried recently at Liverpool a man was charged with harbouring a murderer. It appeared that the police, in an attempt to find the murderer, had allowed the man out on bail and in that way induced him to make a statement. The judge ruled that the statement was inadmissible, and as there was no other evidence against him, he was acquitted. The police no doubt, in both cases, honestly thought the man was guilty and that he ought to have been convicted. But the judges had to put in the balance the greater principle. The freedom of each one of us demands that confessions be rejected if they are influenced by fear or hope held out by the police. So long as the judges hold the balance there will be no police State in England.

I have no time to tell you more now. The other freedoms—freedom of speech, freedom of religion and so forth—must be left to the next lecture : and the place which the juries have played in attaining them. Today I would have you reflect on the part that the judges have played. Men who have come of the common people themselves, they have evolved principles of law which express the spirit of the people—the spirit of freedom : and, with the practical genius of the people they have built up a procedure which protects that freedom more securely than any other system of law that the world has ever seen. These principles and this procedure have spread far beyond the confines of this small island. Go west to the United States, go east to India, go to the countries of the Commonwealth and the farthermost part of the world, you will find that the writ of habeas corpus still runs there—protecting the common man from any encroachment on his liberty by the executive. Think on this and you will realise how great a part the common law of England has played, and still plays, in the destinies of mankind.

FREEDOM OF
MIND AND CONSCIENCE

2

FREEDOM OF MIND AND CONSCIENCE

IN the last lecture I was concerned with personal freedom—a man's freedom to go where he liked on his lawful occasions, his freedom from arbitrary arrest, and from oppression during arrest. Now I come to the freedom of his mind and of his conscience. This is just as important, if not more important, than his personal freedom. To our way of thinking it is elementary that each man should be able to inquire and seek after the truth until he has found it. We hold that no man has any right to dictate to another what religion he shall believe, what philosophy he shall hold, what shall be his politics or what view of history he shall accept. Every one in the land should be free to think his own thoughts—to have his own opinions, and to give voice to them, in public or in private, so long as he does not speak ill of his neighbour : and free also to criticise the Government or any party or group of people, so long as he does not incite anyone to violence.

Although this principle seems obvious to us it is on occasions prone to bring the individual into conflict with the State, or rather with the people who are in power in the State. This country, just as every country, preserves to itself the right to prevent the expression of views which are subversive of the existing Constitution or a danger to the fabric of society. But the line where criticism ends and sedition begins is capable of infinite variations. This is when the practical genius of the common law shows itself. The line between criticism and sedition is drawn by a jury who are independent of the party in power in the State : whereas in the countries of Eastern Europe the line is drawn by people's courts who are only the instruments of the party in power. Just as in the first lecture we saw that personal freedom depended on the remedies for its enforcement, so also freedom of mind and conscience depend on the tribunals which decide upon it.

Let me give you proof of this from our history. Some 300 years ago we had a Star Chamber, which was as much the instrument of the party as the people's courts are in Russia now. The way they approached freedom of speech is well shown by the case of Richard Chambers.[1] He was a silk merchant of London who was, with other merchants, called to the Council Board at Hampton Court because of complaints about the conduct of customs officers. He then said, in the presence of all those at the Council table : ' The merchants are in no part of the world so screwed and wrung as in England '. For those words the Star Chamber fined him £2,000 and ordered him to make submission, that is, to acknowledge and confess his fault. He refused. He said that never till death would he acknowledge any part of it. He was therefore, by their decree, thrown into the Fleet prison. He sought redress by

[1] 3 *State Trials* (5 Charles I, 1629) p. 374.

means of habeas corpus in the King's Bench on the ground that the Star Chamber had no authority to punish him for words only. But the Court of King's Bench refused to release him, saying that the Star Chamber was one of the most high and honourable Courts of Justice. So he suffered in prison six whole years on account of those few words. If you wish for proof that this was solely to get him out of the way, it is provided by what Archbishop Laud said to King Charles about this man Richard Chambers. ' If your Majesty had many such Chambers you would soon have no chamber left to rest in '. All that tyranny was done away with by the abolition of the Star Chamber in 1641 : and Richard Chambers lived to become, during the Commonwealth, an alderman and sheriff of the City of London.

THE SOVIET SYSTEM

Now compare what happened then with what happens in Soviet Russia today. Their Code provides for the detention of persons ' who are a danger by reason of their dangerous associations '[2] : and in order to see whether a person is a danger they look to see what his state of mind is, whether it is a dangerous state of mind or not. They look therefore to his utterances, or even to his thoughts and dreams if they can get information about them. So, for example, in January, 1948, the dancing master of a national theatre in Hungary was arrested for anti-Soviet talk because he was so imprudent as to

[2] Art. 7 of Soviet Penal Code.

disclose that he had a prophetic dream in which he had seen American troops advancing from the north and the west to occupy Hungary.[3]

This recalls our own regulations during the war, when it was an offence to publish matter calculated to foment opposition to the successful prosecution of the war. But the Soviet Code goes much further than we ever did even in time of war. They think it is so important to seize anyone who is a possible danger that they put upon every one in the State a positive duty to denounce traitors. In addition, however, people whose occupations give them special opportunities of hearing dangerous talk, such as waiters, works managers, shop stewards and ship captains, are put under a special obligation to disclose what they hear.[4] Even in time of war we never did that. We never put the hearers of dangerous talk under a legal obligation to disclose it. One can see, of course, the ruthless logic of their system : but it means there is no freedom of speech or of thought. A man may not say what he thinks of the Government to his friends or even to his relations lest they should turn round and denounce him to the authorities.

THE VALUE OF A JURY

Our own experience of the Star Chamber, therefore, coupled with the present happenings in Russia, afford convincing proof that there is no

[3] Reported in newspapers of January 30, 1948. See article by Jean Graven in Le Droit Pénal Sovietique in *Revue de Science Criminelle et de droit penal comparee*, 1948, p. 255.
[4] Art. 18 (2) of Soviet Penal Code.

freedom of speech when the judges are instruments of the party in power. But even when the judges are independent, they may not always see clearly on a question of freedom of speech because of their own predilections on the matter in hand. This is where the value of a jury is most clearly seen. Take the celebrated cases in the eighteenth century on the Letters of Junius. Those letters, you may remember, were open letters addressed to King George III and were very critical of the Government. The burden of the letters was that the King had been misled by the Government. This is one extract showing the sort of thing that Junius said : ' Sir, It is the misfortune of your life, and originally the cause of every reproach and distress which has attended your Government, that you should never have been acquainted with the language of truth, until you heard it in the complaints of your subjects '. It would be interesting to speculate what would happen in Russia if someone said Mr. Stalin was not acquainted with the language of truth !

But in England, in 1770, John Miller, the printer of the words in the *London Evening Post*, was tried before Lord Mansfield and a special jury of the City of London.[5] The charge was seditious libel. Lord Mansfield directed the jury that the question of libel or no libel was a matter of law for the judge, and that the jury was only to decide whether the paper was printed and published. Inasmuch as the paper was obviously printed and published, that direction was in effect a direction to the jury to find Miller guilty.

[5] 20 *State Trials* (10 George III, 1770), 869.

But the jury stood out even against that great judge. The scene is described by Lord Campbell : ' Half the population of London were assembled in the streets surrounding Guildhall, and remained several hours impatiently expecting the result. Lord Mansfield had retired to his house, and many thousands proceeded thither in grand procession when it was announced that the jury had agreed. At last a shout, proceeding from Bloomsbury Square and reverberating from the most remotest quarters of the metropolis, proclaimed a verdict of Not Guilty '.[6]

Thenceforward the defendants were secure, for it was well known that no jury in the City of London would find a verdict against the publisher of Junius, whatever they might be told from the bench as to their functions or their duties. It is now clear that the jury were entitled to do what they did. A jury may always give a general verdict of guilty or not guilty : and no judge can take away that right from them. Parliament has so declared it.[7]

Public Mischief

Since that time we have found no difficulty in criticising the Government ! But we have always to keep on the alert to see that our freedom of speech is not indirectly attacked : for a principle of law has recently been enunciated which is capable of being used to infringe it and has, in fact, on one occasion been so used. I refer to the doctrine that acts done

---

[6] Campbell, *Lives of the Chief Justices*, Vol. II, p. 480.
[7] Fox's Libel Act, 1792.

to the public mischief are punishable by law. This is
a doctrine quite unknown to France and the other
freedom-loving countries of Western Europe where
the law is contained in a written code. They take
their stand on the principle that no one shall be
punished for anything that is not expressly forbidden
by law. *Nullum crimen, nulla poena, sine lege.* They
regard that principle as their great charter of liberty.
In this country, however, the common law has not
limited itself in that way. It is not contained in a
code but in the breasts of the judges, who enunciate
and develop the principles needed to deal with any
new situations which arise.

In recent years the judges have been faced with
acts such as these : A man may call the fire brigade
when there is no fire to attend to : or a woman may
go to the police and tell them an invented story
about being attacked : and thus these public servants
may be diverted from their proper duties. In 1933
the judges declared such conduct to be criminal,
even though it had not previously been expressly
forbidden by law.[8] No one will doubt that it was
criminal, because it was a fraud affecting the public
at large. But unfortunately the judges based their
decision on a wider and much more questionable
ground. They relied on an obiter dictum of a judge
in 1801, who said that ' all offences of a public
nature, that is, such acts or attempts as tend to the
prejudice of the community, are indictable '.[9]

[8] *R. v. Manley* [1933] 1 K.B. 529.
[9] *Per* Lawrence J. in *R. v. Higgins* (1801) 2 East at p. 21. See article
on Public Mischief by Dr. W. T. S. Stallybrass in *The Modern Approach
to Criminal Law*, p. 67.

Now that mode of reasoning is dangerously similar to the reasoning by which the Russian jurists justify the punishment of any acts which are socially dangerous. Starting from the point of view that the interests of the State are paramount, their jurists say that the judges ought to punish any act which is dangerous to the State, even though it is not expressly forbidden. Article 16 of the Soviet Code says that ' if the Code has not made provision for any act which is socially dangerous, it is to be dealt with on the basis, and as carrying the same degree of responsibility, as the offences which it most nearly resembles '. So the only question for their judges is, Is the act socially dangerous ? That is precisely the same test as was stated by our judges in the public mischief case.

The difference, of course, lies in the fact that Soviet judges take their orders from the party in power, and they consider, therefore, that any act is socially dangerous which is dangerous to the party in power : whereas our judges are independent of any party or person, however powerful. The result is that our judges have confined the doctrine of public mischief to cases of making statements to the police of imaginary crimes and such like cases. But there is one exception. In one case where a newspaper had published statements reflecting on the Jewish community as a whole, the printers and publishers were found not guilty of a seditious libel, but guilty of a public mischief.[10] That case is cited in the

---

[10] *R.* v. *Leese and Another*, Cent. Crim. Ct., September 1936. *The Times* September 19 and 22, 1936.

leading text book on Criminal Law as authority for
the proposition that the offence of public mischief
comprises ' such acts as making scurrilous attacks,
whether oral or in writing, on a class of the community, or disseminating rumours calculated to cause
widespread alarm ' :[11] and the same text book
says that it is for the judge, and not the jury, to say
whether the acts are such as to be a public mischief.
If that were the law we should be back to the days of
the letters of Junius, of which I have told you, when
Lord Mansfield said it was for the judge, and not for
the jury, to say whether a publication was a libel.
All the good done by Fox's Libel Act, 1792—which
said that the whole matter was for the jury—would
be done away with by a side wind.

THE TRUE POSITION

That exceptional case has, however, never been
followed : and the true position was restored recently
in a case where the proprietor of a provincial newspaper was charged with seditious libel because he
published an article criticising the Jews.[12]   He
said that they were prominent in the black market,
and so forth. Mr. Justice Birkett pointed out to the
jury how important it was to maintain the freedom
of the press, and the jury, after only fifteen minutes
retirement, unanimously found the proprietor not
guilty.   Afterwards a member of the House of
Commons asked the Home Secretary to revise the law

[11] *Archbold*, p. 1209.
[12] *R. v. Caunt*: *The Times*, October 14, 1947.

so as to prohibit anti-semitic activities of every kind ;
but the Home Secretary did not accede to the
invitation.[13]

The jury in that case, of course, had no antagonism
to the Jews.   They were much more concerned with
the freedom of the press.   It would have been the
same if the editor had published an article criticising
the lawyers, the papists or any other group or party.
The explanation is well put in the report of Lord
Porter's Committee :   ' Much as we deplore all
provocation to hatred or contempt for bodies or
groups of persons, with its attendant incitement to
violence, we cannot fail to be impressed by the danger
of curtailing free and frank—albeit hot and hasty—
political discussion and criticism '.[14]   Now that is
what we mean by freedom of speech and freedom
of the press.   It does not mean that anyone is free to
libel or slander another.   Actions in the court
every day show that.   But it does mean that free and
frank discussion and criticism of matters of public
interest must in no way be curtailed.

But there comes a point at which this country,
and every other country, must draw the line :   and
that is when there is a threat to overturn the State
by force.   When an Australian communist said
recently that ' in a war with the Soviet, the Australian
communists will fight with the Soviet ' it was held
that the words were seditious.[15]   That case was
very much on the border line, as was shown by the

[13] *Hansard*, 1947.   November 20, Written Answer 208.
[14] Page 11.
[15] Reported in *The Times*, October, 1949.

fact that the High Court of Australia was evenly divided on the point. We know, of course, that the Soviet judges would put in prison anyone in their country who said that he would, in case of war, fight with the Americans : but it does not follow that we should do as they would. The right way is to leave it to a jury who can be trusted to draw the line fairly between what is dangerous and what is not.

So far I have spoken only of cases in the criminal courts affecting freedom of speech. But the civil courts have also much to do with it. The principles which they apply are on the whole sound enough. Whilst they protect the individual from being defamed, they hold that anyone is entitled to make a fair comment on a matter of public interest. But the difficulty is in the application of the principles. It is interesting to notice that, as reported in *The Times* a few days ago, Sir Valentine Holmes, K.C.—who probably has had more experience than anyone else in libel actions—said that the defence of fair comment had become one of the most complicated and difficult defences to establish.[16] This should not be so. Nothing is more important than that there should be an independent press entitled to make any honest comment on a matter of public interest, no matter whether it be politics or literature, art or science or anything else.

FREEDOM OF RELIGION

Let me now leave freedom of speech and come to freedom of religion. We have attained to as high,

[16] Reported in *The Times*, October 5, 1949.

if not a higher degree of religious freedom than any other country.   We are free to worship or not to worship, to affirm the existence of God or to deny it, to believe in the Christian religion or in any other religion or in none, just as we choose.

It has taken us a long time to attain this freedom. For many centuries the judges held that Christianity was part of the law of the land, so much so that any denial of the existence of God amounted to the offence of blasphemy punishable in the criminal courts of the land.   You will find it stated in the law books that it is an offence to use language having a tendency to bring the Christian religion or the Bible into contempt ; or to burn the Bible !   The reason for this law was because it was thought that a denial of Christianity was liable to shake the fabric of society, which was itself founded on the Christian religion.

There is no such danger to society now and the offence of blasphemy is a dead letter.   But it is only 30 years ago that the House of Lords made the change. A company was founded for the express purpose of promoting secular doctrine and denying all super-natural belief.   The Lord Chancellor of the day, Lord Finlay, was of opinion that the company was unlawful, because in his view any purpose hostile to Christianity was illegal.   But the majority of the House of Lords took the other view.   They held that the company was lawful and that a legacy to it was valid.   Lord Sumner, in a memorable judgment, said : ' The attitude of the State towards all religion depends fundamentally on the safety of the State and not on the doctrines or metaphysics of those who

profess them. . . . In the present day men do not
apprehend the dissolution or downfall of society
because religion is publicly assailed by methods not
scandalous '.[17]

We have reached the point therefore that whilst
the Christian beliefs still form the foundation of our
way of life, as I trust they always will, they are not
to be enforced by law but by teaching and example.
The same principles were affirmed in 1946 when a
question was raised in the House of Commons as to
the entry into this country of members of the Oxford
Group. The Home Secretary expressed the principle
exactly when he said : ' I am not prepared to apply
religious or political tests to people who desire to
come into this country unless it can be established
that they desire to come here to carry on subversive
propaganda. The common sense of the British
democracy is such that, in the long run, they will
winnow the chaff from the wheat. I wish that the
ancient record of this country as a place of free
speech, where the flow of ideas from all parts of the
world is welcomed, may be maintained '.[18]

Now look abroad and see how the Protestants in
Germany like Pastor Niemoller were treated during
the Nazi regime, and how the Roman Catholics in
Czecho-Slovakia like Archbishop Beran are treated
during the Soviet regime. Why is religion oppressed
in that way in those countries ? Is it not because the
party in power in the State requires undivided loyalty
to itself both in matters of conscience and in matters

[17] *Bowman* v. *Secular Society Ltd.* [1917] A.C. 406 at pp. 466-7.
[18] *The Times*, July 6, 1946.

of politics ? The members of the churches decline to give that loyalty, because they refuse to regard the State as the supreme authority in the matter of conscience. So the party in power regard religion as a danger to themselves and to be suppressed accordingly. That is what happens in countries where the State, or those in power in the State, are irreligious themselves. But when the State itself is religious as this country is—we have not only an established Church, but religious instruction is part of the curriculum in all our schools—there is not the same danger : because the State itself recognises the freedom of the individual in matters of conscience. Hence if we are to maintain freedom of religion, we must keep the State religious. And on this point it is worth recalling Lord Eldon's famous observation ' The establishment is not for the purpose of making the Church political, but for the purpose of making the State religious'.

RACIAL FREEDOM

Closely allied with religious freedom is racial freedom. When you look abroad and see the persecution which the Jews have undergone in Europe on account of their race, it is as well to recall their history here.[19] There were Jews in this country before William the Conqueror came. Indeed there was a law of Edward the Confessor which made them the vassals of the

---

[19] See *Anglia Judaica* or *History and Antiquities of the Jews in England* by D'Blossiers Tovey, LL.D., pub. 1738, and *Re Bedford Charity*, 2 Swanston at pp. 532-3.

King. The Kings treated them as their private property, so much so that Henry III actually assigned and delivered to his brother Richard Earl of Cornwall all the Jews in England as a security for repayment of a debt : and he said they could have services in their own synagogues so long as they held them in a low voice so that the Christians did not hear ! But in the year 1290 Edward the First banished them, because, as the old historians put it, ' they were generally disagreeable to the people'.

PERSECUTION OF THE JEWS

It was at this time only that there could be said to be anything in the nature of a persecution of them in this country but it was sternly suppressed by the law of the land as the following case shows. It is given us by Lord Coke and I take it from the account given by Dr. Tovey in his *Anglia Judaica* which was published in 1738 [20] : ' He says that the richest of the Jews having embarked themselves, with their treasure, in a tall ship of great Burthen ; when it was under sail, and gotten down the Thames, towards the mouth of the river, beyond Queenborough, the Master of it, confederating with some of the mariners, invented a stratagem to destroy them. And to bring the same to pass, commanded to cast anchor, and rode at the same, till the ship, at low water, lay upon the sands : and then pretending to walk on shore for his health and diversion, invited the Jews to go along with him ;

[20] At p. 243.

which they, nothing suspecting, readily consented to ; and continued there till the tide began to come in again ; which as soon as the Master perceived, he privily stole away, and was again drawn up into the ship, as had been before concerted.

' But the Jews, not knowing the danger, continued to amuse themselves as before.   Till at length, observing how fast the tide came in upon them, they crowded all to the ship's side, and called out for help. When he, like a profane villain, instead of giving them assistance, scoffingly made answer that they ought rather to call upon Moses, by whose conduct their fathers passed through the Red Sea, and who was still able to deliver them out of those raging floods which came in upon them : and so, without saying any more, leaving them to the mercy of the waves, they all miserably perished.'

' But the fact coming, some how or other, to be known, the miscreants were afterwards tryed for it, by the Justices Itinerent in Kent, convicted of murder and hanged.'   The justice thus meted out to one of our own people 640 years ago has, we hope, been also meted out to those who in Nazi Germany recently repeated the same offence.

RETURN OF THE JEWS

The number of Jews banished in 1290 was 16,511 : and they never returned until nearly 400 years later. It is sometimes said that there was a Statute of Edward I which banished them and it has never been repealed : but the records of that time are lost.

There is no such statute extant, and if ever it existed, it has long been a dead letter. When the Jews in 1655 petitioned Cromwell to be allowed to return, the Lord Chief Justice and Lord Chief Baron said they knew of no law against it. Cromwell did not actually admit them, but Charles II did. When they returned, they were not under any disabilities other than those common to the dissenters. In the nineteenth century all disabilities were removed : and persons of the Jewish creed and race have held some of the highest offices in the State with the greatest distinction. Their racial freedom is complete.

So also with all other races, it is a cardinal principle of our law, that they shall not suffer any disability or prejudice by reason of their race and shall have equal freedom under the law with ourselves.

It is perhaps easier for us to proclaim racial freedom than it is for other countries such as the United States and South Africa which are faced with a problem with which we have never had to deal. Nevertheless, concerned here as I am with the common law, it is clear beyond peradventure that the common law of England has always regarded a man's race or colour as just as irrelevant in ascertaining his rights and duties as the colour of his hair. If you should go into the Hall of Lincoln's Inn or of any other of the Inns of Court where the students dine, you will see men and women of all races and colour, from all parts of the world, often dressed in the costume of their own lands, come here to study our laws under which all are free.

The Function of the Courts

The freedoms of which I have spoken up till now—are the fundamental freedoms which are necessary to enable each man to develop his personality to the full. These are still fully protected by the laws of England : but in the last resort they depend on the way in which those laws are administered, and it is to this that I would now turn.

The English conception of the function of the Courts of law is very different from that of Soviet Russia. We regard them as standing between the individual and the State, protecting the individual from any interference with his freedom which is not justified by the law. But Soviet Russia regards its tribunals as part of the State machine to carry out State policy. Lenin said that ' The tribunal is the instrument of the proletariat and the working classes ' and this maxim was inscribed in letters of gold in his audience chamber. Soviet Russia rejects altogether the theory of separation between the judicial and the executive power. The judicial power is simply a part of the executive machine.

The Soviets do, indeed, in theory compose their tribunals of representatives of the people, just as our juries are. Their people's courts are composed of a people's judge and two assessors, all supposedly elected by the people : but, as the only candidates are men chosen by the communist party, there is no alternative for the electors. And the way their judges should behave is laid down by M. Vyshinsky in 1934 in his work on ' Penal Procedure ' where he says that the Soviet judge " must not aim solely at legal logic : he must always bear in mind that the law is nothing but the expression of party policy : in practice this means that the Soviet judge, in case of any conflict between the law and the general party line, must unhesitatingly reject a strict application of the law—to which we have seen that he is not, after all strictly bound—in order to give absolute obedience to the party directions which represent, for him, the supreme law."[31]

In addition to these people's courts there is an ' extra-judicial ' system set up to deal with security matters. It is really a police force which investigates cases where people are suspected of acts which are dangerous to the State. After the investigation the State prosecutor decides whether the case is to go before the people's courts, or be dealt with by the Special Procedure. It is said that plain cases, where the guilt of the accused is clear, are sent to the people's courts : and that the other cases are dealt with by the Special Procedure !

UNANIMITY OF THE JURY

Now turn to our own procedure. Here there are no people's courts. There are no servient judges. The judges are entirely independent of the executive, but even they have not the final word. By the constitution of this country a man is not to be found guilty unless twelve of his fellow countrymen—each and all of them—unanimously find him to be guilty. This was

[31] Quoted by Jean Graven (see note 3) p. 260.

settled in 1367 when the Judges of Assize went to Northampton, just as they do to this day.[22] The report says that ' All the jurymen agreed except one who would not agree with the other eleven. They were remanded and stayed there all that day and the next, without drink or food. Then the judges asked the one who stood out if he would agree with his associates : and he said never—he would die in prison first. Whereupon the judges took the verdict of the eleven ' and imprisoned the twelfth. But ' afterwards by the assent of all the justices it was declared that this was no verdict ' : and the twelfth man was set free ' for men are not to be forced to give their verdict against their judgment '. The Chief Justice said that it was fundamental that every verdict should be by twelve ; and the judges who gave judgment on the verdict of eleven were greatly blamed. The reporter tells us in a note that the judges said they ought to have taken the jurors with them in a wagon round the circuit until they agreed.

From that day to this the judges have gone to Northampton and the other Assize towns of England : and never has there been any doubt that a jury must be unanimous. The people of England know this so well that there is no need for the judges to remind them of it. If you go across the border you will find that in Scotland they have juries of 15, that they have majority verdicts, and that they have three possible verdicts ' Guilty, Not Guilty or Not Proven '. In England however, although we compromise on many things, there is one thing that we will not

[22] Y.B. 41 Edward III, 31, 36 ; S.C. 41. Ass. 11. 2 Hale 297.

compromise on and that is our freedom. The freedom
of no one of us is to be taken away on a compromise ;
he must either be found Guilty or Not Guilty : and
that by the verdict of each and all of a jury of his
fellow-men : and by no one else.

THE INDEPENDENCE OF THE JURY

Time and time again the jury has been found to be our
safeguard, not only against harsh laws, but also against
political prejudice and legal formalism. Their independence was not achieved without great struggles.
For some 300 years the judges used to claim the right
to fine and imprison jurors if they brought in a
verdict contrary to the evidence or against the judge's
direction in point of law. But this was brought to
an end in 1671 by the celebrated case of the Quakers
William Penn and William Meade who preached in
Gracechurch Street before 300 people and were
charged with unlawful and tumultuous assembly.[23]
The Recorder of London directed the jury that on
the evidence the Quakers were guilty but the jury
acquitted them. The Recorder thereupon imposed
upon the 12 jurors a fine of 40 marks apiece because
he said they had not obeyed his direction in point of
law. They refused to pay and the Recorder committed
them to prison. But the jurors, headed by their
foreman Edmund Bushell, brought their habeas
corpus and it was agreed by all the judges of England
(one only dissenting) that this fine was not legally set
upon the jury for they were judges of matters of fact ;

[23] *Bushell's Case*, Vaughan 135. 2 Hale p. 313.

and, as for the allegation that they had disobeyed the
direction in point of law, ' this mended not the matter,
for it was impossible any matter of law could come
in question, till the matter of fact was settled and
stated and agreed by the jury, and of such matter of
fact they were the only competent judges.'   So the
jurors were set free.

Thus was brought to an end the practice of
punishing jurors—a practice which Sir Thomas Smith
had long before in the reign of Queen Elizabeth
declared to be very violent, tyrannical and contrary
to the liberty and custom of the Realm of England.
The principle so established by plain Edmund Bushell
and his companions is fundamental in our constitution.
It still happens sometimes that a jury give a verdict
contrary to the judge's direction but he cannot
punish them for it.   For instance, years ago at the
Winchester Assizes a sailor was charged with
murdering a girl on Southampton Common.   The
defending counsel submitted to the jury that it was
a case of manslaughter, not murder, but the judge
took the view very strongly that there was no case of
manslaughter to leave to the jury and told them it
was not open to them to find manslaughter.   As the
sailor had admittedly killed the girl, this was
equivalent to a direction that the jury should find him
guilty of murder.   The Hampshire jury came back
and, in the teeth of the judge's direction, returned
a verdict of manslaughter.   The judge then turned
to the jury and said ' Get out of that box. You're not
fit to be there.   Get out, you're not fit to be a jury.'
If the judge had remembered the ruling about the

jurors in the Quaker's Case he would probably not have spoken thus. Even as it was, he could not do anything about it. He had to accept their verdict. Even assume, what you have no right to assume, that the sailor was guilty of murder, and that the wrong verdict was given, nevertheless it is much more important that the jury should be free to give their verdict according to their conscience than that a judge should have power to dictate it to them.

If any proof was needed of this, another trial which took place in that very Castle at Winchester 250 years ago would provide it. Dame Alice Lisle was charged with high treason because she had given some food and a night's lodging to two men who had fought with Monmouth. It was the first case tried by Judge Jeffreys on that bloody assize. It was one of the most disgraceful trials in our history. He browbeat the jury unmercifully. When they had been out a long time, he sent a messenger to tell them, that if they did not come back with their verdict at once, he would adjourn and they would have to be locked up all night. They came back and said they did not think there was sufficient proof. But Judge Jeffreys thundered at them again. Some say that they returned three times and refused to find a verdict until Jeffreys in a transport of rage threatened them with an attaint of treason : then most reluctantly they found her guilty and she was put to death on a scaffold in the market place at Winchester.

The trial of Dame Alice Lisle, however, has remain burned into the memory of the people : and you will not find a jury in England which will not, if they think right, hold their view against the strongest judge. These instances show what a decisive effect the jury have on the law. Their presence means that the legislators and the judges have to keep the law in accordance with the views of the common people of England, for assuredly they will not give effect to a bad law. So when juries refused to convict men accused of stealing when the punishment for it was death, the law had to be altered. So now when juries are prepared to convict for murder most foul, but oft-times not for unpremeditated killing, it may be that the law will have to be altered so as to divide homicide into three categories of murder, manslaughter and unlawful killing. The presence of the jury also means that the judges have to keep the law simple so as readily to be ' understood ' of the people. Legal formalism and hair-splitting are thus kept in check.

You should not believe from what I have said that the juries habitually disregard the views of the judge. Far from it. The common law of England is, on the whole, in full accord with the good sense of the people. The judge states it simply and clearly to the jury and they loyally accept it from him. They then apply the law so stated to the facts of the case. He in turn has great respect for their good sense in dealing with the facts. So there is a mutual confidence between them and it is this confidence which makes the system work so well. It holds fairly the scales between the man who is accused and the community which accuses him. It keeps the balance. If there were ever any possibility in this country of the judges being influenced by the party in power in the State, as happened in Nazi Germany and happens now in Russia, there would yet stand, between the accused and his oppressors, a jury of his fellow countrymen. To this day, when a man accused of serious crime is put in charge of the jury, it is in words which have come down through the centuries : ' To this charge he has pleaded not guilty and puts himself upon his country, which country you are.' All our past struggles are bound up in that one sentence. He entrusts his liberty to a jury of his fellowmen. So in the last resort do we all.

THE FRENCH MODE OF TRIAL

But the jury system depends on the men who take part in it. It works in the English-speaking countries because of the temperament of the people, their sane good sense, which is not to be swayed unduly by emotion or prejudice. It does not work in the Latin countries with their mobile temperament, easily moved to pity or hate. The verdicts there given by juries were often fantastic. So in France, since 1941, after more than a century of trial, it has been abandoned, at least in the form we know it. At a criminal trial in the Cours D'Assize there are now three judges and seven jurors who all sit together on the bench. There is no summing-up by the judge to jury and no distinction between facts and law. The three judges and seven jurors all retire to consider the case together and all decide not only on the question of guilt but also on the sentence. They

may decide by a majority but do not disclose that fact.
The result is to give the professional judges a larger
degree of control over the jurors than obtains in
England. It is their way of keeping the balance and
no doubt suits their country. But it would not do
here.

Indeed if you examine the mode of trial in this
country and compare it with the mode of trial in the
Continental countries, you will find at almost every
stage a difference in the way in which the balance is
kept. In England whenever there is a doubt, the
scale goes down in favour of the accused. The
' golden metwand ' by which all our rules of evidence
and procedure are measured is that no man shall be
found guilty unless his guilt is proved beyond
reasonable doubt. Even if he is in fact guilty, we
care not. His freedom is not to be taken away unless
he is proved guilty. In France the general principle
is in theory the same. It is specifically laid down in
the Declaration of the Rights of Man that every man
is presumed to be innocent until he is proved guilty.
But the rules of evidence and procedure all tend to
put the balance the other way.

Let me illustrate this from the previous convictions
of the accused. In England the prosecution are not
as a rule allowed to put before the jury any evidence
that the accused is a man of bad character or been
previously convicted of any crime. The evidence
before the jury is confined to matters within the
witness's own knowledge directly relevant to the
crime with which the man is charged. But in France
the trial starts with an examination of the accused by

the Presiding Judge, in the course of which his previous convictions are all brought to the knowledge of the court, a thing which is never done in England until after he has been convicted and then only for the purpose of deciding the sentence. It is regarded here as quite irrelevant in deciding whether he is guilty or not. But in France the court of trial has from the outset a description of his conduct at school and at work or in the forces, the reports of his superior officers and his employers, his previous convictions and so forth. If any such evidence were admitted in England, it is certain that many would be convicted here who are now found not guilty. Views may differ as to which system is better but it does at any rate show a difference in balance which corresponds to the temperament of the people.

In France after dealing with the man's life history the Presiding Judge goes on to deal with the details of the offence. He has already read all the depositions and the evidence which have been collected, and has often taken a provisional view that the man is guilty. Then he puts his views to the accused, to our eyes more as a prosecutor than as a judge, so that to all the world the appearance is given that the man will be found guilty unless he manages to exculpate himself. This examination, so conducted, has led observers to suppose that in France a man is presumed to be guilty unless he proves himself to be innocent. This is not so. It just shows the difference in balance.

As the witnesses are called, there appears a still greater difference from our English practice. The

Code lays down that a witness is not to be interrupted. So each witness makes a statement which he may have prepared beforehand, containing not only direct evidence of what he himself saw or heard but also all kinds of hearsay, what his own views on the matter are, and so forth. Many in this country were no doubt surprised to read that in Paris in a recent trial for libel in the book *I Chose Freedom*, prominent English politicians and public men were called to give evidence ; for it would seem that according to our notions, there was no relevant evidence they could give. But it is said that in France ' in all sensational trials every one is called who may be counted upon to make a really good speech, journalists, politicians, and professors of philosophy being in particular demand.' [24] A witness may be asked a few questions but he is not tested by cross-examination as we know it. It would be regarded by the average Frenchman as unfair to the witness.

Contrast that with our English system. The right of cross-examination is regarded by us as so vital that a verdict would be upset if a party had not had the opportunity of cross-examining the witness. When cross-examination is properly conducted, it is not only not unfair to the witness, but it is a most valuable instrument in ascertaining the truth. It is known that distinguished Continental judges who had the opportunity of observing the cross-examination by Sir David Maxwell Fyfe of the witnesses at Nuremberg have changed their views about the desirability of cross-examination.

[24] Wright on French Criminal Procedure, 45 L.Q.R. 98.

Coming to the close of the trial there is yet another significant difference. There is no summing up in France by the judge. The advocates have their say, and then judges and jury consider their verdict together. Whereas here the judge reviews the whole case, for and against the prisoner, throughout insisting that he is not to be found guilty unless the case is proved beyond reasonable doubt.

CONCLUSION

In making these comparisons, we no doubt think our system is better but we ought always to remember that it is the system which suits the temperament of our people. It would not necessarily be the best system for other peoples. Remember that the jury system has proved a failure in France. But one thing is quite clear. The system which has been built up by our forefathers over the last 1000 years suits our people because it is the best guarantee of our freedoms. The fundamental safeguards have been established, not so much by lawyers as by the common people of England, by the unknown juryman who in 1367 said he would rather die in prison than give a verdict against his conscience, by Richard Chambers who in 1629 declared that never till death would he acknowledge the sentence of the Star Chamber, by Edmund Bushell and his eleven fellow-jurors who in 1670 went to prison rather than find the Quakers guilty, by the jurors who acquitted the printer of the Letters of Junius, and by a host of others. These are the men who have bequeathed to us the heritage of freedom. It is their spirit which William Wordsworth interpreted so finely when he wrote :—

' We must be free or die, who speak the tongue
    That Shakespeare spake ; the faith and morals hold
Which Milton held : In everything we are sprung
    of Earth's first blood, have titles manifold.'

JUSTICE BETWEEN MAN AND THE STATE

3

JUSTICE BETWEEN MAN AND THE STATE

ITHERTO I have discussed freedoms which were uncontroversial. Now I have come to those which are controversial, particularly, freedom of property and freedom of contract. The judges of England in the nineteenth century were inclined to protect these freedoms with as much vigour as they protected a man's personal freedom or his freedom of speech. In this they were wrong. They weighted the scale too heavily in favour of the rights of man. So much emphasis was laid on his rights that they seem to have forgotten that he had any duties. In the middle of the nineteenth century you would find judges proclaiming that ' Fraud apart, there is no law against letting a tumble-down house.'[1] That meant that a landowner could put up ramshackle back to back houses with no sanitation, and let them for whatever rent he could get : and no matter that the roof leaked, and the damp rose up the walls so the tenant and his family fell sick, or the stairs gave way so that he broke his leg, nevertheless the law gave no remedy. The judges who laid down this law were only conforming to the political thought of their time. You would not find the judges of today subscribing to such a law if they were free to decide the contrary.

[1] *Robbins v. Jones* (1863) 15 C.B.N.S. 221.

But the trouble is that, once a rule of law has been established by one generation of judges, their successors are bound to follow it.[2] They may pare it away, and try to mitigate the consequences, but they cannot reverse it altogether. That can only be done by Parliament. So you will find the balance being kept by Parliament. Have any of you any doubt now that a landlord ought not to be allowed to build ramshackle houses, or that, if he lets a house for people to live in, he ought to see that it is fit for the purpose ? There are laws now to ensure that, but they are laws made by Parliament,[3] not by the judges.

The extent to which judges in the nineteenth century carried rights of property seems to us today to be almost incredible. They allowed owners of property to use it as they liked, even if it meant injuring others. There was a celebrated case about the Bradford water supply.[4] The water for the town percolated underground through the land of a property owner named Mr. Pickles. He wanted the Corporation to buy his land, but they refused. So in revenge he sank a shaft in his land which not only reduced the flow of water but also discoloured it. His real object was to show that ' he was master of the situation and to force the Corporation to buy him out at a price satisfactory to himself.' The House of Lords held he was entitled to do it. He was entitled to use his property as he pleased. Lord Macnaghten said ' He prefers his own interest to the public good.

---

[2] *e.g. Otto* v. *Bolton* [1936] 2 K.B. 46.
[3] See Housing Acts, 1909-1936.
[4] *Bradford Corporation* v. *Pickles* [1895] A.C. 597.

He may be churlish, selfish, and grasping. His conduct may be shocking to a moral philosopher.' But it was not unlawful. Have any of you any doubt in this twentieth century that it ought to be unlawful ? The feeling of most people today is that rights of property carry with them responsibilities and must not be abused. Yet there is that extreme law laid down by the House of Lords which is bound by its own decisions. The only power that can alter it is Parliament.

But just as the property owners were entitled to prefer their own interest to public good, so also anyone who had a bargaining lever was able to exploit it for his own benefit. It was all done under the name of ' freedom of contract.' However harsh were the terms of any contract, the judges enforced it. They said ' you have this paramount public policy to consider—that you are not lightly to interfere with this freedom of contract.'[5] Oh, what abuses were not covered by this catchword ' freedom of contract ' ! It mattered not to the judges of that day that one party had the power to dictate the terms of a contract and the other had no alternative but to submit. If he had submitted to it, however unwillingly, he was bound. So in the days of housing shortage, when men with families were looking in vain for a furnished room in which to live, the law, as laid down by the judges of the nineteenth century, would have us believe that there was freedom of contract between the landlord and the tenant. Have you not heard of a

[5] *Printing and Numerical Registering Co.* v. *Sampson* (1875) L.R. 19 Eq. 462 at p. 465, *per* Jessel M.R.

landlord saying to a prospective tenant, ' Take it or leave it,' which is equivalent to saying ' pay my price or go on the streets.' What freedom is there for the tenants there ? Whenever you find that one person has a virtual monopoly of essential supplies or services, you will often hear the same words ' take it or leave it ' which really mean ' Accept my terms or go without my essential service.' The law as laid down by the judges of the nineteenth century compels the courts to enforce the terms thus imposed, however unreasonable they may be.

The abuses did not stop there. You would find innocent parties bound by harsh terms of which they knew nothing until their powerful opponent produced them, so to speak, ' out of the blue.' That was the fate of some unfortunate people who went by an excursion train and were injured by the Railway Company's negligence.[6] The Company disclaimed any liability because on the back of the ticket there were words printed that it was issued subject to the conditions in the Company's time tables ; and that if the passengers had looked at the time tables, they would have found there was a condition exempting the Company from liability for their own negligence. That defence succeded.

The Duty of the Individual

So the story might be continued. The judges of today would no doubt be glad if there could be introduced into the law some principles which could remedy

---

[6] *Thompson* v. *L.M. & S. Ry. Co.* [1930] 1 K.B. 41.

such abuses : but the law is settled and they can do nothing. The utmost that the judges have been able to do is to lay on every man the negative duty that he ought not to injure his neighbour without just cause or excuse. They have not been able to lay on him any positive duty to help or benefit his fellow-men. The law therefore falls far short of the Christian precept that you should love your neighbour. As Lord Atkin said ' The rule that you are to love your neighbour becomes in law, you must not injure your neighbour ; and the lawyer's question, Who is my neighbour ? receives a restricted reply.'[7]

But if the hands of the judges are tied, the hands of Parliament are not : and the significance of the social revolution of today is that, whereas in the past the balance was much too heavily in favour of the rights of property and freedom of contract, Parliament has repeatedly intervened so as to give the public good its proper place. Whether the balance has swung too far, I do not say. That is not my province. All I am concerned to tell you is how the balance is being kept. It is being kept by statute after statute which interferes with the rights of property and freedom of contract. The property owner must keep his houses fit for human habitation and must not charge more than the standard rent. The landlord of furnished rooms must only charge a reasonable rent. And so forth. Furthermore statute after statute now puts on men the positive duty of doing good to their neighbours and to the community at large. The farmer must farm his lands in accordance with the

[7] *Donoghue* v. *Stevenson* [1932] A.C. 562 at p. 580.

rules of good husbandry, the school proprietor must provide proper instruction, the doctor and the dentist must provide efficient service, and so forth.

The principle which runs through all our recent legislation is that those who engage in a public calling, or in providing essential supplies and services, must not carry them on simply for their own private profit, but must provide adequate and efficient service at reasonable charges for the good of the public generally. Previously a positive duty to do good and faithful service rested only on the direct servants of the Crown. Now it extends to a great many more. England does not merely *expect* every man this day to do his duty. It *requires* every man every day to do it.

REMEDIES AGAINST THE CROWN

This striking re-orientation of the duties of the individual to his neighbour and to the community is only matched by the duties which have been imposed on the community towards the individual. Do you realise that until two years ago the law gave no remedy as of right to any individual as against the State ? If the War Office agreed to buy boots from a Northampton manufacturer and later refused to take them, it could not be sued except with the permission of the Attorney-General. If an army driver drove his lorry at a dangerous speed on the wrong side of the road and killed a man, his widow and family had no claim against the War Office but only against the private soldier, who would have no money with which to pay damages. These rules were not based on reason but on historical grounds which were long out of date. They were often got over in practice because in cases of breaches of contract the Attorney-General always did give his fiat ' Let right be done ' ; and in cases of negligent driving, the War Office always did pay any damages which were awarded against the driver. And so forth.

But these devices did not ensure justice. That was pointedly shown when the military authorities, who had laid a minefield in some sandhills, did not keep it properly fenced : and some boys, when looking for their tennis ball, ran into the minefield and were injured. It was impossible for the parents of the boys to point to any particular officer and say he had done wrong ; and so they had no remedy at common law. When the case came before the House of Lords in 1946 Lord Simonds pointed this out and said ' No one who has any experience of these matters will doubt that legislation on the subject of proceedings against the Crown is long overdue.'[8]

In the very next year, 1947, the Crown Proceedings Act, 1947 was passed. It makes the Government Departments liable to be sued for their breaches of contract and for the wrongs of their servants just as any other contractor or employer would be. This Act is of profound significance in our constitutional law. It does a great deal to keep the balance as between the individual and the State. No longer is the Crown a privileged person before the courts. It is under the same common law duties and has the same common law responsibilities as any

[8] *Adams* v. *Naylor* [1946] A.C. 543.

other corporation or person in the land. The full effect of the Act has perhaps not yet been fully realised. It certainly means that if doctors and dentists under the National Health Service do their work negligently so that their patients are injured, the State is liable to pay damages. It may mean that if the inspectors, who hold local inquiries, should make defamatory statements the State may be liable in damages for slander. Whether it means that the State is liable if its officers exercise their executive powers oppressively or spitefully, I would not care to say. All this has yet to be worked out in the courts.

But you must note that the Crown Proceedings Act does not put positive duties on the State. It simply puts the State, like the individual, under the negative duty not to injure another without just cause or excuse. But the question that arises is, what about positive duties and responsibilities? The ordinary man, as we have seen, is being put under positive duties to do good to his neighbour and to the community. Is not the State also under positive responsibilities to its citizens?

THE RESPONSIBILITY OF THE STATE

One hundred years ago the responsibility of the State was very narrowly interpreted. It only provided the bare necessities of the community as a whole, such as defence against aggression, the maintenance of order, and the provision of workhouses for the destitute. When a man grew old and unable to work he had to be kept by his children or go to the workhouse. If he fell sick and could not pay for medical treatment, he had to rely on charity. If he was injured at his work and perhaps disabled for life by some slip or miscalculation on his own part, or by the fault of his mate, he got no compensation from his employer, although it was in the employer's service and on his work that he was injured. The law, I regret to say, did little more than provide a defence for ' rights of property ' and ' freedom of contract '. It did not recognise any right to freedom from want. All was left to the charitable instincts of the few.

The social revolution of today has changed all that. Parliament has put on the State the positive responsibility of seeing that everyone is provided with the necessities of life. Act after Act has put on the State the responsibility of providing for the sick and poor, the fatherless and the widows. Act after Act has put upon local authorities the duty of providing for the welfare of their inhabitants. Act after Act has created public corporations, put them under the control of the State and charged them with the efficient working of essential services. The principle that runs through all the recent legislation is that the State is responsible for seeing that all the supplies and services which are necessary for individual well-being are available to all.

THE NEW TRIBUNALS

It comes to this, therefore, that the social revolution of our time has resulted in the creation of a

great number of new duties of a kind unknown before
—positive duties of the individual towards the State
and of the State towards the individual. I am not
concerned with the political thought which has
produced these duties but with the legal machinery
which has been evolved for enforcing them. In the
old days the legislature nearly always entrusted to the
ordinary courts of law the task of ascertaining and
vindicating the rights and duties which it created.
And in the early days of this social revolution it did
the same. But the enforcement of the great majority
of the new duties is now entrusted to Government
Departments or to tribunals whose members are
appointed by the Government Departments.

It would be tedious to take you through all the
many tribunals now in operation. All I am concerned
to point out is that they exercise what is essentially
a judicial function. Their task is to ascertain and
vindicate all these new rights and duties which have
been given or imposed by Parliament. This judicial
function must be distinguished from the administrative
functions of Government Departments. When a
Minister exercises powers which have been conferred
on him by Parliament, as for instance to acquire land
or lay out a new town, he is exercising administrative
functions. He is not adjudicating on existing rights
and duties, but is creating new ones. Those I will
deal with later, but confining myself to judicial
functions, the question is why has Parliament made
this radical departure ? Why has it entrusted all
these judicial functions to new tribunals instead of
to the courts ? The reason is—we must face it

squarely—that the ordinary courts are not suited to the task—or, if you will, the disputes are not suitable for decision by the courts. Some of the disputes are so numerous that the courts would not have sufficient judges to cope with the amount of work involved. Other disputes involve so much specialised knowledge that they need specialist judges to deal with them. And, more often than not, expedition and economy are essential factors which, it is thought, the courts do not provide. Perhaps the most decisive consideration, however, is the feeling that the new rights and duties are better dealt with as part of an administrative system. So Parliament has set up administrative tribunals to deal with them.

The French System

There is no doubt that the ordinary courts have watched this development with a jealous eye. But if they looked across the Channel they would realise that there is no cause for alarm. The French people have, for more than one hundred years, had two sets of courts. The ordinary courts administer the law as between subject and subject. The administrative courts administer the law as between the subject and the State. The ordinary courts take their law from the civil Code. The administrative courts have a system of case-law which has been developed by the judges. Some of the reasons which led to the creation of these administrative courts are the same as those which have led us to the creation of new tribunals : but there was an additional reason which does not apply

here. The State there seems to have suspected the
ordinary courts of a spirit of hostility towards it so
that it could not obtain justice in them ; with the
result that it has gone much further than we have in
taking away work from the ordinary courts.

Most of the disputes in France between an
individual and the State—or any public undertaking—
are dealt with by the administrative courts. For
instance, if anyone is injured by the fault of any public
servant in the course of his service, the injured
person has no remedy in the ordinary courts. His
only remedy is in the administrative courts. This
applies to people injured in railway accidents, or by
the local dust carts, and so forth : because they all
form part of the public services. Whereas we, of
course, allow an action in the ordinary courts for
any wrongs of that kind, whether done by a servant
of the Crown or of a public authority.

If the French system did not adequately protect
the individual as against the State, it would be a
serious criticism : but all the evidence seems to show
that in some respects it affords him better protection
than our own system. An interesting contrast is
offered by the way in which the two countries deal
with explosions in munition factories. The
administrative courts in France hold that, if anyone
in a factory is injured by an explosion, the risk should
fall on the State : whereas the English courts hold
that, apart from national insurance benefits, the State
is not liable unless the injured person proves that
there was negligence on the part of some servant of
the Crown, which is often an impossible task. In

other words, the English courts still adhere to the
nineteenth century doctrine that there should be no
liability without fault, whereas the French administrative courts adopt the view that ' justice requires
that the State should be responsible to the workman
for the risks which he runs by reason of his part in the
public service '.[9]

An equally interesting contrast is afforded by the
way in which the two countries protect the rights of
public servants.   In France the administrative courts
are recognised as the guardians of the public servants
as against their employers, the State.   When,
therefore, the Rector of Strasbourg Academy was
asked to take up other duties and thus relieved of his
post, without, in fact, any new duties being given to
him, the court regarded it as a disguised move to get
rid of him and gave him redress.[10]   But in England
the public servants have no remedy in the ordinary
courts or before any tribunal.   The ordinary courts,
as a rule, hold that public servants can be dismissed
at pleasure :   and if and in so far as they are given
statutory rights and liabilities, the final arbiter is often
the Minister.   So recently, when a local government
officer sought to establish a claim to superannuation in
the courts, he found to his dismay that his own local
authority were entrusted with the initial decision of
his right, and that his only recourse from them was an
appeal to the Minister.[11]

Indeed, comparing the two systems, it would

[9] Compare *Read* v. *Lyons* [1947] A.C. 156 with L'Arret Cames,
Anglo-French Legal Conference, 1947, p. 85.
[10] Anglo-French Legal Conference, 1947, p. 87.
[11] *Wilkinson* v. *Barking Corp.* [1948] 1 K.B. 721.

seem that the French system of administrative courts is worthy of more respect from people in this country than it has sometimes received. So far from granting privileges and immunities to public authorities, the French administrative courts keep them in order and exercise a supervision and control over them which is more complete than anything we have here. These courts have the confidence of the administration because they are staffed by men who understand the administrative problems : and they have the confidence of the public because they are independent of the administration and have proved themselves vigilant to protect the interests of the individual. I do not say that this system would suit us here. One of its drawbacks is that often a party may not know whether he ought to go to the ordinary courts or to the administrative courts : and they have had to set up yet another court to decide those conflicts. But the lesson which can be learnt from the French system is that a separate set of courts dealing with administrative law is not necessarily a threat to the liberty of the individual, but may actually afford him much-needed protection.

There is no doubt that the new tribunals in England do constitute a set of administrative courts : but they have grown up in so haphazard a fashion that it is difficult to fit them into any recognisable pattern : and one of the most important tasks of the lawyers of to-day is to mould them into a coherent system of courts which will keep a just balance between the claims of the community on the one hand and the freedom of the individual on the other.

There is no need for the ordinary courts to be jealous of the new tribunals. It should be recognised that they are a separate set of courts dealing with a separate set of rights and duties. Just as in the old days there were the ecclesiastical courts dealing with matrimonial causes and the administration of estates—and just as there was the Chancellor dealing with the enforcement and administration of trusts—so in our day there are the new tribunals dealing with the new rights and duties as between man and the State. The great need is to work out the principles and procedure which should govern these tribunals.

The Independence of the Tribunals

The most important principle of all to establish is that the tribunals should be independent of the executive. If this is vital for the ordinary courts it is even more vital for the tribunals and it is more difficult for them to attain. In many of the cases which come before the tribunals you will find that the Government Department or the local authority concerned has already come to a conclusion on it adverse to the individual. A soldier will have had his claim to a pension rejected by the Minister of Pensions, an injured workman will have had his claim for industrial benefit rejected by the insurance officer, the Agricultural Executive Committee will have formed the view that the farmer is not farming his land properly, the Medical Executive Council will have thought the doctor should not be continued in the Health Services, and so forth. The man is therefore appealing against the official view and if the tribunal is to command his confidence it should be composed of men who can approach it from a completely independent standpoint.

It is at this very point that a fundamental divergence from the ordinary courts appears. If there is one thing above all others of which the Englishman can be sure it is that the judges are independent of the executive. They are paid a salary and have a security of tenure which ensures their independence. But the same guarantees are not often offered to members of tribunals. They are usually three members, one of whom is a lawyer and the other two laymen chosen for their special experience or knowledge, and, more often than not, none of them has any security of tenure. The chairman is, as a rule, only appointed for a fixed period of longer or shorter duration, or may be just for one sitting, with the result that, if those in power think he is not suitable, he will not be appointed again : and he is paid a comparatively small salary or fee which is not commensurate with the importance of his task. The laymen are similarly placed. Mark you, however, the tribunals on the whole do their work admirably. The members of them give their services more out of a sense of public duty than for reward—just as the justices of the peace do—and so long as the proper standards are maintained, there is no reason why they should not receive the confidence of the public. The important thing is to see that the proper standards are maintained and particularly that the Government Departments do not lay down the law to them.

The uneasiness which has been felt about the tribunals is undoubtedly due to the fact that their development is closely linked with the enforcement of policy : and on that account their independence is suspect. It is felt, rightly or wrongly, that, as the Government Departments appoint the members, they have power indirectly to influence the decisions of the tribunals. Indeed, one of the advantages claimed for the tribunals is that greater uniformity of decision can be obtained in them than in the ordinary courts. If that is so, it can only be done by circulars or directions from the Government Departments, explaining their view of the law which the tribunals should apply. Uniformity achieved by such means is bought at too high a price. The tribunals have to decide issues between the individual and the State : and, if the scales are to be kept even, it is vital that the law they apply should be laid down by a Superior Court and not by a Government Department.

THE ATTITUDE OF THE JUDGES

The independence of the tribunals is reduced to vanishing point in cases where, as sometimes happens, an appeal from the tribunal is only to the Minister and not to the courts. An appeal to the Minister means, of course, an appeal to the officials of his Department : and so the officials have the last word, even on points of law. So drastic a departure from all our traditions could only be justified if the ordinary courts had not kept pace with current thought : and were apt to retard, rather than advance, the social reforms which the new age has introduced. That, indeed, has been suggested. One Minister of the Crown, in an unwise moment, when he refused an appeal to the courts, gave as his reason that he feared the ' judicial sabotage ' of his plans.[12] This was an unfair criticism of the judges. There would have been more point in it if it had been directed against some of the rules which the judges inherited from the nineteenth century. They used undoubtedly to interpret statutes too literally, and they were unduly tender to freedom of contract : but the defects have been and are being corrected, by the judges themselves, so far as they are able, and by Parliament so far as they are unable. Thus whereas previously ' there was no law against letting a tumble-down house ', Parliament has put landlords under an obligation to keep their houses fit for human habitation and the judges have interpreted this so as to make them repair broken sashcords, replace defective tiles and maintain the houses in a good standard of repair.[13]

In these days no reproach can be levied at the judges that they have not kept pace with the times. The judges of England have no politics and always carry out the intentions of Parliament as expressed in the statutes or to be inferred therefrom. The position here is very different from what it was at one time in the United States where, you will remember, President Roosevelt's new deal was nearly thwarted by a written Constitution and by judges who were out

[12] *Hansard*, July 23, 1946, p. 1983.
[13] *Summers v. Salford Corp.* [1943] A.C. 283.

of touch with the times : so much that it was only by the appointment of new judges to the Supreme Court that the legislation became effective.

The Soviet System

Some solution must therefore be reached whereby the independence of the tribunals is assured. The French have managed it in their administrative courts and we must do the same. We must avoid the experience of Russia. After the revolution of 1917 all the ordinary courts were overthrown. The revolutionaries in Russia regarded the existing judges as reactionary, and they so distrusted them that they created new tribunals consisting of a people's judge with two people's assessors. The members of these tribunals are theoretically elected by the people but are, in fact, nominated by the party in power— because there are no other nominations. If they do not perform their tasks to the satisfaction of the party they may be dismissed or, at any rate, not re-elected. They are entrusted with the task of enforcing the Soviet idea of justice which, in theory, looks well. The idea is that every individual should be provided with the essentials of life free : and that, in return, every individual should be under a duty to do his part in producing those essentials.

All this wears a familiar likeness to the new rights and duties, and the new tribunals, which we have created here. But in working them out in Russia and her satellite countries the balance has gone all wrong. The scales have descended so heavily in favour of the duty of the individual towards the State that it has been forgotten that he has any rights. The State has become identified with the party in power : with the result that the tribunals have simply become the instruments for enforcing the will of the party in power. We must see to it that that does not happen here. The new rights and duties, which the new age has brought in, have no doubt to be decided by tribunals, but they must be tribunals who are completely independent and do not look at the case through the spectacles of the Government Departments.

THE WAY TO ACHIEVE INDEPENDENCE

How, then, is this independence to be achieved ? The answer is by giving a right of appeal on a point of law to a Superior Court which is itself known to be independent. The law then which the tribunals will apply will be the law laid down by the Superior Court and not by the Government. Parliament has realised this, for if you study the Statute Book you will find that Parliament has of late repeatedly given a right of appeal to a Superior Court. Appeals to a Superior Court have been given, for instance, from the War Pensions Tribunals, Local Appeal Tribunals for Insurance Benefits, Disciplinary Committees of Marketing Boards and the Lands Tribunals. The appeal is not always to the High Court ; sometimes it is to permanent Commissioners as, for example, under the National Insurance Acts—where the Commissioners have an independence and security equal to that of a judge. But whatever form the Superior Court takes, so long as it is a court which is entirely independent of the executive, it means that the tribunals themselves are independent also.

UNANIMITY OF TRIBUNALS

Let me give a few illustrations of the value of a right of appeal to the courts ; and perhaps you will forgive me if I take most of them from the Pension Appeal Tribunals, because I am more familiar with them than some of the others. A fundamental point in these tribunals, and of all other tribunals for that matter, is whether the three members have to be unanimous or not. When the Pensions Appeals Tribunals were set up there was nothing in the statute about it, but someone or other seems to have told them, or at least they somehow got the impression that they could decide by a majority ; but that they should not disclose the fact, lest it might make the disabled man dissatisfied. So for years they acted in that way until, in some cases, acute difference arose. A familiar instance was when the cause of a disease was unknown. The Ministry doctors used often to admit that they did not know the cause of the disease but, nevertheless, would assert that it could not be due to war service. This might convince two members of the tribunal. But the third member might argue that if they did not know the cause, how could they assert that, beyond reasonable doubt, it was not due to war service. Cases such as this made it imperative to decide whether the tribunal could decide by a majority or not. The High Court held that the tribunals had no right to give a majority decision.[14] They must be unanimous, because it could not be said that the disease was proved beyond reasonable doubt to be not due to war service when one of the members felt so strongly in the man's favour that he dissented from it : and it could not have been intended by Parliament that questions of fact should be finally decided against the man by a majority of two to one.

Similar problems arise in the case of other tribunals, and it is important that some recognised procedure should be established. If the decisions of tribunals on questions of fact are to be final and conclusive without any appeal to a Superior Court, then they should be unanimous, just as the decision of a jury must be unanimous. It is apparent that if the lawyer chairman, and the two lay representatives, who usually represent opposing interests, are unanimous, the decision will command the respect, if not the agreement, of both the contending parties. But if a majority decision were to be allowed, no one would have great confidence that the decision is right : because if a fair-minded man feels so strongly about a case as to dissent, he is nearly as likely to be right as the other two. If a majority decision is permissible therefore, there should be an appeal to a Superior Court on a question of fact as well as of law, just as there is from the decisions of justices of the peace, unless the matter at stake is so small that there should be no appeal at all.

[14] *Brain and Wilkes* v. *Minister of Pensions* [1947] K.B. 625.

Admissibility of Evidence

Then again, in the course of their work all tribunals are faced with the question of what evidence they should accept. They are not bound by the rules of evidence which are applied in the ordinary courts. Those rules have sometimes been considered too exacting in that they require the best available evidence to be produced and exclude all hearsay. But there are dangers in having no rules at all, because it may result in the tribunal deciding against a man without hearing any evidence at all. Quite recently a Rent Tribunal reduced the rent payable to a lady without hearing her evidence at all and the High Court quashed the decision and ordered the members of the tribunal themselves to bear the costs.[15] So also, at one time, the Pensions Appeals Tribunals used often to accept the Minister's point of view about a case—as, for instance, his view whether a disease could be attributable to war service or not—without requiring it to be supported by the evidence of any doctor.[16]

Many cases have occurred before various tribunals where the tribunal has received information adverse to one of the parties and actually acted on it without giving him an opportunity to deal with it. For instance, a Rent Tribunal recently reduced the rent of some modern flats because, on their inspection, they noticed that some of the rooms were not more than eight feet high—whereas if they had given the landlord an opportunity of dealing with it they would

[15] R. v. *Kingston-upon-Hull Rent Tribunal, ex p. Black*, 65 T.L.R. 209.
[16] *Moxon* v. *Minister of Pensions* [1945] K.B. 490.

have realised that they had all been passed by all the authorities before they were built.[17] These mistakes were corrected by the High Court. But these cases do show that it is not possible to dispense with rules of evidence and procedure altogether. Rough justice may become so rough that it ceases to be justice.

QUESTIONS OF LAW

Apart from general questions of these kinds common to all proceedings before tribunals, vital questions may arise in regard to the particular subject-matter involved. Quite recently a district auditor attempted to surcharge a man, who was not a member of the local authority, but the managing director of a company which had a contract with it. The Court of Appeal held that he had no power to do it.[18] Other illustrations could be taken from the treatment of war pensions. Before 1943 a disabled man had himself to show that his incapacity was due to war service : but in 1943 it was laid down by Royal Warrant that if he was passed fit when he went into the army and later discharged unfit, it was to be presumed that his incapacity was due to war service unless the contrary was proved beyond reasonable doubt. The tribunals for some time did not appreciate the full import of that compelling presumption. If they could find nothing in the man's medical history to account for his incapacity they used often to assume that it was not attributable to

[17] *R.* v. *Paddington and St. Marylebone Rent Tribunal, ex p. Bell* [1949] 1 K.B. 666.
[18] *Dickson* v. *Hurle-Hobbs* [1948] 2 K.B. 95.

war service. But the medical records were, of course, not always complete, and, in any event, the tribunals did not, as a rule, have before them the complete file but only extracts made by the Ministry of Pensions, which might, by an oversight, omit something material. So, in one case where a widow not only gave evidence herself but also provided evidence from her husband's officer and comrades that he had suffered from a particular gastric trouble during service, a tribunal refused to accept the evidence because the medical history contained nothing about it.[19] If there had been no appeal to the court she would not have got her pension.

It must be remembered that in many of the cases the tribunals have not the benefit of legal argument. Indeed, sometimes the parties are forbidden to employ barristers or solicitors. This may be justified on the ground that it greatly reduces the expense, but it deprives the tribunal of a great advantage. Many of the mistakes that do occur are no doubt the result of this. I know of nothing which is so essential to a right decision as to have the benefit of arguments which put forward all that can be said on each side. At any rate, in those tribunals where argument is often lacking, there should be an appeal to a Superior Court where full argument can be had.

One more word : every tribunal should give a reasoned decision, just as the ordinary courts do. Herein lies the whole difference between a judicial decision and an arbitrary one. A judicial decision is based on reason and is known to be so because it is

[19] *Lee* v. *Minister of Pensions*, 2 Pension Reports 1901.

supported by reasons. An arbitrary decision, for ought that appears, may be based on personal feelings, or even on whims, caprice or prejudice. If the tribunals are to command the confidence of the public they must give reasons.

WHERE THERE IS NO APPEAL

Let me now turn to tribunals where there is no appeal to a Superior Court. There are, I fear, many of them still. There is the Agricultural Land Tribunal, which decides whether a farmer should be dispossessed on the ground of bad husbandry. If it decides against the farmer, he has no appeal to the courts. The author of the leading textbook on Agricultural Holdings says, in the latest preface, that ' access to the King's Courts has, with a few exceptions, been taken away from both landlord and tenant of an agricultural holding.'[20] So also with Rent Tribunals. In none of them is there an appeal to the courts.

If any proof was needed that there should be an appeal to a Superior Court it is provided by cases which have been recently reported. One of them will undoubtedly rank as a leading case.[21] It arose in connection with the new tribunals which have power to fix the rent of furnished lettings. The underlying principle of this legislation is that the landlord has in his control an essential supply, and it is his duty only to charge a reasonable rent. Not only the tenant, but the local authority, can compel

[20] W. Hanbury Aggs, *Agricultural Holdings Acts.*
[21] *R.* v. *Paddington and St. Marylebone Rent Tribunal, ex p. Bell* [1949] 1 K.B. 666.

him to perform this duty. They can apply on their own initiative to the tribunal to fix a reasonable rent and, thereafter, the landlord is tied down to this amount. There is no appeal to the courts from the decision of the tribunal, nor even to the Minister. But the courts, as you will hear, have some degree of control so as to prevent them exceeding or abusing their jurisdiction.

Let me, however, go on with the story. There is, as you know, a large block of flats in Paddington called Park West. In 1947 two of the tenants referred their tenancy agreements to the tribunal and got their rents reduced. Thereupon the Paddington Borough Council referred 302 of the other flats in the building straightway to the tribunal. In eight of them the tribunal reduced the rents. Several points arose in the case, but the only one for present purposes is this : When the tribunal reduced the rents, they did not give the landlords any credit for the fact that the landlords were providing a lift, a swimming pool and many other amenities for the tentants, which were obviously of considerable value. The tenancy agreements contained nothing to bind the landlords to supply those amenities, and so the tribunals thought that, in consequence of recent decisions, they could not take them into account. Now that is a typical point of law upon which the High Court could have ruled, if there was a right of appeal to the court. It was obviously desirable that there should be an authoritative ruling upon it : so the Solicitor-General did invite the court to express an opinion on it for the guidance of tribunals ; and the court did so. But if that had not been done, the tribunals might have gone on indefinitely acting on a wrong view of the law—all because the statute did not provide for any appeal to the courts.

It should be clearly understood that, although the High Court has some degree of control over the tribunals it is not such as to enable it to correct many of the faults or injustices which may arise, unless the statute gives an appeal. The High Court proceeds on the footing that if Parliament has thought fit to entrust jurisdiction on all these new matters to new tribunals without any appeal from them, then, so long as the tribunals do not exceed or abuse their jurisdiction, the High Court should not interfere with them. If a tribunal should come to a wrong conclusion on the facts, or, indeed, if there is no evidence on which it could come to its conclusion, the High Court cannot interfere : nor, if the tribunal comes to a wrong conclusion in point of law, can the High Court interfere.[22] So long as the tribunal keeps within its jurisdiction, and is not guilty of any flagrantly unjust procedure, its decision is final both on facts and law.[23]

APPEAL TO A MINISTER

Let me now turn to cases when there is an appeal from the tribunal to the Minister. Instances are the

[22] *R.* v. *Ludlow* [1947] K.B. 634. See also 49 L.Q.R. 94, 419.
[23] It seems that any tribunal *may* state a case for the opinion of the court on a point of law : but it is doubtful if it can be compelled to do so unless a statute so provides, see *Walsall* v. *L.N.W.Ry.* (1878) 4 A.C. 30 ; *R.* v. *Southampton J.J.* [1906] 1 K.B. 446 ; and 63 L.Q.R. 214. A ' Speaking ' order, *i.e.*, an order which gives reasons may be quashed for error in law.

doctors and dentists tribunals. The papers recently reported the first decisions of these tribunals. They show that these cases may give rise to points of law of some importance. For instance, when a dentist was struck off the list for what were, no doubt, adequate grounds—at any rate, he did not appeal—the tribunal added that he had ' on more than one occasion adversely criticised the National Health Service and attempted to bring it into disrepute '. Now suppose that had been the only ground for striking him off, would it be an admissible ground ? At any rate, the dentist's only appeal would be to the Minister who is responsible for the Health Service.

In another case where a doctor had been guilty of behaviour of which the tribunal took an extremely serious view, the tribunal held that it was a single incident and he should not be struck off on account of it. They added that they were of opinion that ' no negligence of the doctor in any way caused or contributed to the death '. Now suppose they had come to the opposite conclusion, and struck him off because his negligence had caused the death. The doctor's only appeal would be to the Minister. No more serious verdict could well be given affecting a professional man. Issues of that kind are repeatedly tried in the courts before a judge and jury and often reach the Court of Appeal. It is a new thing to have questions of this kind authoritatively determined by a Minister—which means by the officials in his Department.

Conclusion

Looking at these cases, is it not clear what the remedy is? It is to bring the cases where there is no appeal to a Superior Court into line with those cases where there is an appeal. There should be a Superior Court, which is able, not only to see that the new tribunals keep within their jurisdiction, but also to review their decisions on points of law and, in proper cases, on questions of fact. The Superior Court should be either a High Court judge, as in the War Pensions Appeals, or a Commissioner, as in Insurance Appeals : and this court should be able to give leave to appeal in any case where there is a principle of importance involved or there are other special circumstances to justify it. The decision of the Superior Courts should be published and form a body of administrative law. The Superior Courts should not be treated as a separate set of courts similar to the administrative courts in France. They should be welded into the Supreme Court of Judicature. It will then be apparent to all that the new tribunals administer the law just as much as the other courts of the land. Their task of doing justice as between the subject and the administrative branches of government is just as important as the task of doing justice between man and man. All alike, tribunals and courts, are concerned with maintaining the rule of law without which there is no freedom for any of us. We must see to it that the stream of British freedom—which has been kept clear by the decisions of the judges—does not perish in the bogs and sands of departmental decisions.

THE POWERS OF THE EXECUTIVE

4

THE POWERS OF THE EXECUTIVE

I COME last to the most significant feature of our time—the increasing powers of the executive. I need hardly remind you of the extent of these powers. They touch the life of every one of us at innumerable points : and they are an inseparable part of modern society. No one will deny that we could not have reached our standards and way of life without them. Our railways and roads could not have been built unless the public authorities had power to acquire land compulsorily. The slums would still be with us, if it had not been for the many clearance orders which have been made. Our towns and countryside would have been much more disfigured than they are, if there had been no town and country planning. The housing difficulties could not have been met except by the use of powers of requisitioning ; and so forth. At every point, however, these powers involve interference with private rights and interests : and, granting that private rights must often be subordinated to the public good, it is essential in a free community to strike a just balance in the matter.

There is a vital difference between the powers now under consideration and the rights and duties which were the subject of the last lecture. Those were rights and duties which could be ascertained and vindicated by courts or tribunals, however imperfectly. But now I am concerned with powers of public authorities over which no court or tribunal has jurisdiction, so long as they are not exceeded or abused. The Government Department which requisitions my house, or compulsorily acquires my land, does not exercise a judicial function. It is exercising a statutory power and performing an administrative function. Once the power is exercised the legal position is transformed. The Government takes possession of my house and I am turned out, receiving a compensation rent : or it becomes the owner of it and I have but a claim to its value. New rights and duties are thus brought into being by the exercise of the power : and once it is exercised the courts must enforce them. But over the power itself the courts have little control. They cannot say to a Minister that he should requisition this house or should not requisition that one : or that he should not acquire this piece of land but should take some other piece. All that the courts can do is to see that the powers are not exceeded or abused.

But this is a most important task. ' All power corrupts. Total power corrupts absolutely '. And the trouble about it is that an official who is the possessor of power often does not realise when he is abusing it. Its influence is so insidious that he may believe that he is acting for the public good when, in truth, all he is doing is to assert his own brief authority. The Jack-in-office never realises that he is being a little tyrant.

Let me first put on one side cases of actual

corruption. Those can be dealt with by the criminal law. For instance, the other day a manufacturer applied for a building licence. An official of the Ministry of Works visited the site and made a very favourable recommendation to his superiors : and he said to the manufacturer ' If you get the licence it will cost you ten per cent.'. The manufacturer was anxious to get the licence and he realised that, unless he agreed to the proposal, he might not be successful : so he agreed to pay the sum. Later he received the licence and the official immediately got in touch with him, wanting his ten per cent. That case, of course, finished up at the Old Bailey. I trust that there are not many cases of corruption of that kind, but they can safely be left to the criminal courts.

Let me next put on one side cases where the officials actually exceed their powers. Sometimes, for instance, the public authorities will slip into their schemes something which goes beyond anything that Parliament intended[1] : and sometimes they will try and delegate to other people powers which Parliament intended they should exercise themselves. That happened, for instance, where a county council, which had power to licence films, purported to delegate its power to the British Board of Film Censors, which was an unofficial body appointed by the firms who let out films. The court held that the county council had no authority to delegate its functions to that unofficial body.[2] Anything like that which goes beyond the powers conferred by

[1] *Ex p. Davis* [1929] 1 K.B. 619 ; *Ex p. Yaffé* [1931] A.C. 494.
[2] *Ellis* v. *Dubowski* [1921] 3 K.B. 621.

Parliament is, of course, invalid. It will not be enforced by the courts and will, if necessary, be quashed. Cases of that kind do not often arise nowadays : for you will find that the public authorities are usually well advised on the precise scope of their powers, and comply with all the necessary formalities.

Let me come, then, to the real question with which this lecture is concerned, and that is the misuse of power. One of the most important tasks of the courts is to see that the powers of the executive are properly used, that is, used honestly and reasonably for the purposes authorised by Parliament and not for any ulterior motive.

This problem bears considerable likeness to those which faced the courts in the great constitutional struggles of the past. When the King—Charles I— ordered the county of Buckinghamshire to provide a ship of war of 450 tons with 180 men, guns, gunpowder and all things necessary ; and sought to levy ship-money on John Hampden for the purpose, Mr. St. John, who was counsel for John Hampden, admitted that the King had power to give the orders. He admitted that the King was the sole judge of dangers from foreigners and had power to command the inhabitants of each county to provide shipping for the defence of the realm. But his contention was that the power had been used by the wrong medium or method ; that it could only be exercised with the consent of Parliament, which had not been obtained ; and therefore it was unlawful. His contention did not prevail with the court, as it ought to have done, and it needed a civil war to establish it.

The problem before us to-day is not so clear-cut. It is more subtle, as is to be expected in a more complex society : but it is in principle the same, and it must be solved by the courts and not by a civil war. For to-day the executive have great powers over the lives and property of every one of us. No one will dispute that the powers exist, for Parliament has granted them, but the question is what remedy the courts provide if they are misused or abused.

An Englishman's House is His Castle

Let us consider, then, the power to enter a man's house against his will : for this is a power which has been greatly extended of late. It is a power which we must watch with care, because, next to our personal freedom, we value most the freedom of our homes. ' An Englishman's house is his castle ' we say : and our feelings about it were well summed up by the great Earl of Chatham when he said ' The poorest man may in his cottage bid defiance to all the forces of the Crown. It may be frail—its roof may shake—the wind may blow through it—the storm may enter— the rain may enter—but the King of England cannot enter—all his force dares not cross the threshold of the ruined tenement '.[3] These proud words take their legal origin from Magna Carta, when King John promised that no free man should be disseised of his free tenement except by the law of the land. The freedom of an Englishman's house was there put on an equal footing with his personal freedom.   Just as

[3] Brougham, *Statesmen in the time of Geo. III.*

the executive could not deprive a man of his personal freedom except when the law permitted, so also the executive could not enter his house except in accordance with the law.

POWER OF SEARCH

This did not mean, however, that the King or his officers never had any right at all to enter a man's house. All that it meant was that they had no prerogative right to enter. A householder could not, of course, be allowed to abuse the freedom of his house so as to give refuge to malefactors and thieves. The law therefore allowed the King's officers to enter in order to arrest a felon who was taking refuge there. But the officers could not break down the outer doors unless they complied with very strict conditions. They had to state their business and demand admission.[4] When you read in your story books of the King's officers knocking at the door and demanding admission by saying ' Open in the name of the King ' you must not suppose that was an idle formula. It was essential. And they had to specify their business. If they had a warrant they had to say so : ' We have a warrant for the arrest of John Smith, fugitive from justice '. If, after all that, the householder still refused admission, they could break down the door in order to get in. But even so, they had to be sure that the fugitive John Smith was there : for if he was not they still had no right to enter.[5] The householder

[4] *Semayne's Case*, 1 Sm.L.C. (13th ed.) 104, 114.
[5] 2 Hale P.C. 117.

could resist them by force : and if they did get in, he could sue them for damages in an action for trespass.

So you see the householder was not allowed to harbour criminals : and he was also bound to keep the peace in the house. If there was a bloody affray going on there ; or if there was a disorder in a tavern late at night, a constable could demand entry ; and, if refused, he could break open the doors so as to keep the peace.

But those were the only cases where the judges allowed a constable to enter. They did not allow any of the King's officers to enter a man's house simply in order to search it to see if anything unlawful was going on there. Even if the officers suspected that there was a wicked plot being hatched there to blow up the Houses of Parliament ; or, to come to lesser offences, even if they suspected that counterfeit coins were being made there or banknotes forged, they had no right to enter or to search the house. And they could not better the position by going to a magistrate and asking him to grant a search warrant : because a magistrate had no power to grant a search warrant except to search for stolen goods.

In this situation the executive government assumed to themselves the power to enter a man's house. The Secretaries of State claimed the right to issue general warrants for the search of premises. They were really looking after their own interests because they claimed to be able to search for seditious libels : and they regarded any attack on themselves as a seditious libel. For nearly one hundred years they went on issuing these general warrants and no publisher or bookseller disputed their right. But they had then to reckon with John Wilkes. He published the *North Briton*, attacking the Government. Thereupon the Secretary of State, in accordance with the usual practice, issued a general warrant to seize his papers and told the messengers that ' all must be taken, manuscripts and all '. Accordingly all was taken, and John Wilkes' ' private pocket book filled up the mouth of the sack '. John Wilkes then challenged the validity of these general warrants in the courts. He succeeded in showing them to be illegal. The judges held that no one, not even a Secretary of State, has power to issue a search warrant in order to see if incriminating material can be found.

Now no one can doubt that the judges went too far in protecting the freedom of a man's house. It meant that a house could be used as a cover for all kinds of offences and yet the constables could not go in, and the magistrates could not grant a search warrant. The community were not sufficiently protected. So the balance was restored by Parliament. In a great many cases now Acts of Parliament permit magistrates to grant search warrants so as to enable the police to enter and see if a house is being used for unlawful purposes, such as coining, betting and so forth. But a policeman cannot, as a rule, enter of his own head. He cannot enter a house, without the owner's consent, simply to see what is going on there. He must go to a magistrate and show reasonable grounds for thinking that an offence is being committed there. So far as the powers of the police are concerned it can safely be said that the freedom of a man's house has not been infringed any more than is absolutely necessary for the protection of the public.[6]

NEW POWERS OF ENTRY

But it is different with the new powers of entry and search which the new age has ushered in. Enforcement officers of the Minister of Food may enter shop premises, inspect all the goods in it, require the shopkeeper to produce his books and so forth. Factory Inspectors, Sanitary Inspectors, Town Planning Officers may all enter all kinds of premises for their various purposes. Officials of the Ministry of Supply may enter your house to see if you are doing research into atomic energy. Officials of the Agricultural Executive Committee may come on your land to see if you are farming it properly.

The granting of these powers of entry is a complete departure from the principles hitherto in force in England. The powers conferred on these officers are greater than those conferred on the police. It is not necessary for these officers, as it is for the police, to go to a magistrate and satisfy him that a search should be allowed. It is not necessary for them to show reasonable grounds for thinking that an offence has been committed. It is not necessary for them to hold a specific authority in respect of specified premises. All that is necessary is that the inspector

[6] The cases of *Elias* v. *Passmore* [1934] 2 K.B. 164, and *Thomas* v. *Sawkins* [1935] 2 K.B. 249 have been adversely criticised by jurists, but they seem to be reasonable and just decisions, so long as they are not extended beyond their proper ambits.

should produce, if required, a duly authenticated authority, which means a general authority issued by an official in a Government Department, authorising the inspector to enter premises of the kind in question.

Powers of this kind were conferred to a limited extent before the war, but were greatly increased during it, and many have been made permanent. Now no one will, I imagine, dispute that it is often necessary that officers of the executive should have a power to inspect. If workmen are to be protected from injury by unfenced machines, a factory inspector should be enabled to go into a factory and require the machinery to be fenced, before an accident happens, rather than wait till after it has happened. If your drains are out of order and likely to contaminate the whole district, a sanitary inspector should have power to enter and see what is wrong. If a merchant is making large profits by selling goods in excess of his quota, or at prices above the maximum, a food enforcement officer should be entitled to go in and inspect the books, rather than that the merchant should be able to flout the law, at the expense of the tradesmen who abide by it. Indeed, if the various Acts and Regulations are to be obeyed the only way of enforcing it may be by giving wide powers of entry and search to the executive.

ABUSE OF POWER

But allowing for all this, what is to happen if these officers abuse their powers? It is easy to see how they might be abused. An officer who enters to inspect a factory or shop may, by keeping his eyes open, learn much about the manufacturing processes there and the trade secrets, or he may glean commercial information which would be useful to a competitor ; or he may outstay his welcome by spending more time there and occupying more room than any reasonable necessity could warrant. Is there any remedy at law for such abuses ? If there is none our freedom would indeed be seriously impaired. After all, the arguments by which the powers of entry are given here are much the same as the arguments by which the police States of Eastern Europe justify their oppressive powers. The State Rules must be obeyed and there must be a right of entry to see that they are obeyed. But the difference is that in this country there is a remedy for abuses of these powers ; and that may be one of the reasons why comparatively few abuses have occurred.

The judges more than three centuries ago laid down principles which are as applicable to-day as they were then. In 1610 six carpenters went into a common inn in Cripplegate and bought and drank a quart of wine and paid for it ; but they afterwards had another quart and some bread and refused to pay for it. The judges held that, as it was a common inn, the six carpenters had authority by virtue of law to enter it, but if they afterwards abused that authority as, for instance, if they stayed an unreasonable time, they became trespassers from the beginning.[7] So also to-day, if any of these various officers act unreasonably and so abuse the powers of

[7] *Six Carpenters' Case*, 1 Sm.L.C. (13th ed.) 134.

entry given to them by law, their entry will become unlawful, and they will be liable for trespass, and so will their masters, the Crown. Now that is a very important case, which may provide the key to the principle by which the courts can ensure that the new powers of the executive are not abused. The principle is that when powers are given for the furtherance of the public interest, the judges will not allow them to be used oppressively or unreasonably.

POWER OF REQUISITION

Not only however is a power of search given in these days to the executive. There is often a power given to them to take possession of a man's house itself. It is done by way of requisition. This great power was never in the old days allowed by the judges to anyone, not even to the King himself, even in time of war. The King in this respect had only the same right as any man in the Realm. He could make trenches or bulwarks if that was immediately necessary for the defence of the Realm ; just as in the recent war bulldozers dug anti-tank trenches across the counties of England. But he could not take mills for making gunpowder or houses for administrative purposes unless the owner consented, and then he had to pay reasonable compensation.

All that is altered now. During the recent war Parliament gave the executive power to take possession of houses for war purposes ; and this power has been continued in peace-time for the purpose of dealing with the housing shortage and other social problems.

This power of requisitioning can not only be exercised by the officials in the Government Department concerned ; but these officials can also delegate the power to anyone else ; and they have repeatedly done so. They have, for instance, conferred on the town clerks of local authorities the power to requisition houses in their district, and so forth. This shows how far we have got from the old ideas of the rights of property. Nowadays if any of these officials think it necessary or expedient to take any house for any of the extremely wide purposes mentioned in the various Acts, they are entitled to do it. The subordination of private rights to the public good is complete.

No doubt the situation in the country has been so difficult that it has been necessary to give these drastic powers to the executive. Owners of houses could not be allowed to leave them empty whilst homeless people walked the streets. It was very right and proper that the local authority should be able to take these properties to house those in need, and on the whole they have used their powers with moderation and restraint. But what if the powers are abused, is there no safeguard ? Is the individual completely at the mercy of the executive ? Have the courts no say in the matter ? The answer is Yes. Just as the courts will interfere if the power of search is abused, so they will if the power of requisition, or any other power, is abused.

ABUSE OF POWER

They have in the first place insisted that the officials must always, on request, disclose the authority under which they act. This point arose in the case of an interpreter of languages who had a house at Blackpool which he wanted to sell as it was too large for him. When he had got a purchaser and agreed to sell it with vacant possession, the town clerk stepped in and requisitioned it. The town clerk no doubt took the view that, as the owner had agreed to give vacant possession, he did not need it for his own occupation, and it should therefore be requisitioned to house the people on the Blackpool waiting list. But of course the inevitable happened. As soon as the purchaser heard of the requisition he called off the deal. So the owner told the town clerk that he would go into occupation himself. But the town clerk did not take any notice of that. He proceeded with the requisition and got the Ministry of Health in London to back him up. From their point of view, no doubt, the requisitioning was justified. They probably thought that the owner did not really want to go into occupation himself, but just wanted to avoid the requisition. But they did not disclose the authority under which they acted. When the owner's solicitors asked for a copy of the circulars under which the town clerk acquired power to requisition, he was told that the circulars could not be made available to the public. If the circulars had been produced, they would have shown that, as soon as the owner said he would go into occupation himself, the town clerk ought to have withdrawn the requisition. It was nearly six months before the owner's solicitor got a copy of the circulars ; but, of course, when he did get them, he was able to point out the flaw, and the requisition was held to be bad.[8]   The judges sternly condemned the executive for withholding the circulars.   Just as a policeman must, if required, produce the warrant authorising him to search my house, so must a town clerk if required, produce the authority authorising him to requisition it.

That is one instance of the abuse of powers.   It is easy to see other ways in which the powers of requisition might be abused.   At one time, for instance, when landlords in some big towns were extorting extravagant rents from tenants, the local authority stepped in and requisitioned the houses and let them at a reasonable rent.   But that made them the judges of whether the rents were extravagant or not.   So also when builders in different parts of the country, who had been granted licences to build houses on condition that they sold them at a certain price, began to take illicit bribes from purchasers, over and above the purchase price, the local authorities stepped in and requisitioned the houses just before they were completed.   But that made them judges of whether the builders were acting illegally or not.   Supposing that in some of these cases, as may well have happened, the local authorities were quite wrong and there was no foundation for their suspicions, would not a grave injustice have been done to the builder and the purchasers ?

There are principles at hand to deal with such abuses.   They are to be found in the cases on

---

[8] *Blackpool Corp.* v. *Lockyer* [1948] 1 K.B. 349.

compulsory purchase. This is, like requisitioning, a case where private rights of property are subordinated to the public good, but it is of much longer standing. The vast public works of the last 100 years could never have been made without the power of compulsory purchase. It is a great power, and a necessary power, for an executive to have. But the courts will interfere if it is abused. That was shown in a case which came before the Privy Council. The Corporation of Sydney had power compulsorily to acquire land for development purposes : and proceeded to acquire land in the middle of Sydney which was likely to increase greatly in value. It was proved that they did not really intend to develop the land themselves, but to sell it at a profit. The Privy Council held that they could not take the land for that purpose.[9] Now that is a very important case. The Corporation had the best of motives. They did not see why the private owners of property should take all the increased profit which they had done nothing to earn. It ought to go to the public, by way of the Corporation. But they were wrong. The powers given to them for the purpose of development could not be used for an ulterior or different purpose, no matter how praiseworthy it may be.

Drawing on this case, and on cases about powers conferred on individuals,[10] you will gradually see developing in England the principle that the courts will always be prepared to look into the purpose with which the executive exercise their powers and will

[9] *Sydney Corp* v. *Campbell* [1925] A.C. 338.
[10] *Vatcher* v. *Paull* [1914] A.C. 372, 378 ; 64 L.Q.R. at p. 277.

not allow them to be used for any purpose other than that for which they are conferred.

Détournement de Pouvoir

This principle has been found necessary to protect the individual in all the freedom loving countries. It has been much developed in France by the administrative courts under the name of ' détour-nement de pouvoir,' that is, the misuse of power. Those courts insist that a public authority must exercise its powers genuinely in the public interest. The courts will therefore look into the intention with which the act was done : and if it was done with a motive, or for an end, other than that for which the power was conferred, it will be held to be bad. An instance which they give in their books is where a newly elected mayor dismissed the municipal servants, one and all. He gave them the regular notice required by law, but nevertheless the administrative courts held it to be an abuse of his power, because it was manifestly taken from political motives and had no relation to the interests of the public services.[11]

That case shows the way in which the French approach these cases. In order to see what the intention of the public authority is, the courts will look at the act itself, and if they find it to be cynical or maladroit, they will hold it to be a misuse of power. And their courts have gradually enlarged the scope of ' détournement de pouvoir ' so as to keep pace with the needs of the times. For instance

[11] Anglo-French Legal Conference, 1947, pp. 114-5.

whereas previously the administrative courts absolutely refused to inquire into the reasons for
refusal of a road traffic licence by the Road Board,
they will now do so and will set the refusal aside if
it was done with the wrong motives.[12]

Now we are developing the same principle here
along parallel lines. Just as the French mayor was
not entitled to dismiss all the corporation servants
at once, so here the Poplar Borough Council were
held not entitled to pay all their workers a minimum
wage of £4 a week, irrespective of whether they were
worth it or not.[13] And just as the French courts
looked to see why the road traffic licence was
refused, so here the Brighton Corporation was held
not to be entitled to refuse an omnibus company
permission to bring chara-bancs into the town, simply
because it disliked the way in which the same
company ran its buses from Hove into Brighton.[14]
A most important case which applies the same
principle is the case of which I told you in the last
lecture when the Paddington Borough Council
referred 302 flats in Park West to the Rents Tribunal
so as to get the rents reduced. They made no sort
of inquiry or investigation before they did it. They
did not consult the tenants to see if they wanted their
rents reduced. In some cases the flats were empty,
in other cases they were unfurnished, in others the
names of the former tenants were given and so forth.
The courts held that the conduct of the Borough

[12] Anglo-French Conference, p. 89.
[13] *Roberts* v. *Hopwood* [1925] A.C. 578.
[14] R. v. *Brighton Town Council*, 32 T.L.R. 239.

Council, in referring the flats in that way, was not a genuine exercise of their powers, and that all the references were bad.[15] The Lord Chief Justice gave this illustration : Suppose a Corporation which had power to put up a fence in the street to protect the passengers, put up a close-boarded fence 10 or 12 feet high along the edge of the path, their action would be invalid because it was not the sort of thing which Parliament ever intended they should do.

These cases show how the courts insist on the powers being exercised genuinely for the purposes conferred by Parliament and not for any ulterior purpose. If they are exercised in a way which is plainly unreasonable, then the court will infer that it was not a genuine exercise of the power. If they take into account things which they ought not to take into account, or if they do not take into account things which they ought to take into account, so also the court will interfere.

PROPER USE OF POWER

This does not mean that the courts will interfere with a public authority which exercises its powers genuinely in the public interest. It is not the use of powers, but the misuse of them, which the courts will intervene to prevent. So when the Wednesbury Council gave permission to open cinemas in the town on Sundays, but made it a condition that children under 15 should not be admitted at all, with or

[15] R. v. *Paddington Rent Tribunal, ex p. Bell* [1949] 1 K.B. 666.

without an adult, the court declined to interfere.[16] In such cases the courts proceed on the principle— similar to that of the French administrative courts— that, when powers are entrusted by Parliament to a public authority, it is not for the courts to say how they should be exercised, so long as they are not abused.

That happened in a case where the Bristol Corporation proposed to purchase compulsorily an estate for the purpose of putting up houses. The estate had already been developed by a family of father and sons who were builders. Before the war they had made roads and sewers on the land and built some houses on it. They had actually, by arrangement, helped the Corporation with the main sewers and bus routes leading to and from the estate. Then the war stopped further work. After the war they were just about to start building again when the Corporation stepped in and decided to acquire the estate compulsorily. The Corporation thought it would be better if they developed it themselves as part of their larger scheme rather than let the builders develop it. The builders appealed to the courts to upset the compulsory purchase order, but with no success. The claims of the builders, however meritorious, had to be subordinated to the public good.[17]

Public Inquiries

Parliament has, however, in most of these cases made provision for seeing that the powers are not exercised

---

[16] *Associated Pictures* v. *Wednesbury* [1948] 1 K.B. 223.
[17] *Green* v. *Minister of Health* [1948] 1 K.B. 34.

without a proper consideration of individual rights. Whenever a scheme of development is proposed which will interfere with private rights of property, you will find that Parliament insists that before any order becomes effective there should be a public inquiry into the matter. So whether it be a slum clearance scheme, a town planning scheme or a new town scheme, an inspector from the Ministry comes down to hold a public inquiry. I have in my time attended many of them, often I fear for owners of back-to-back houses, or blocks of tenement buildings which were far below modern standards : and the most the owner could say was that he was prepared to reconstruct them so as to make them fit for human habitation. It was as a rule a hopeless task. The inspector invariably gives a courteous hearing, visits the site and reports to the Minister. The officials in the Department then consider the matter and ultimately the order or scheme is made operative, or disallowed, as the case may be.

Now there have been several cases in the courts about this procedure and I fear that there has been a good deal of confusion of thought about it. The task of the inspector has sometimes been regarded as almost a judicial function, as if he could only act on evidence and could not receive any information from one side without giving the other an opportunity of dealing with it, and so on. The truth is that the inspector at a public inquiry of this kind is not exercising a judicial function. He is not a judge and does not behave like one. He does not rule on the admissibility of evidence nor give any judgment. He cannot commit for contempt of court. Neither he nor the advocates or witnesses have any absolute privilege in what they say. He is not there to hear and decide. He is only there to hear and report. His report is made confidentially to the Minister. The parties do not see it. The Minister must no doubt consider it, but he is in no way bound by it. Nor is he confined to it. If he chooses to act on other information, he can do so : or even if he chooses to act without any evidence, he can do so.[18] He is not even bound to bring an open mind to bear on the matter. He may act on his preconceived ideas, if he likes, so long as he genuinely considers the objections that have been made.

All this would seem quite shocking if the Minister were exercising judicial functions. But that is where the difference comes. The exercise of powers for the public good is not a judicial function but an administrative one : with which the court will only interfere if the Minister acts in a disingenuous way, or, as the French put it, in a way that is cynical or maladroit. This is shown quite clearly by the famous Stevenage case.[19] In that case you may remember the question was whether the order made by the Minister of Town and Country Planning for a new town at Stevenage was valid. There had been an inquiry by an inspector and a report to which no objection could be taken, but it was said that the order was bad, because, before the Minister had considered the objections, he had gone down to Stevenage and made

[18] *Robinson* v. *Minister of Town and Country Planning* [1947] K.B. 702.
[19] *Franklin* v. *Minister of Town Planning* [1948] A.C. 87.

a speech. He had said ' I want to carry out in Stevenage a daring exercise in town planning— ' This provoked some of the audience to jeers, and he went on ' It is no good your jeering ; it is going to be done.' Applause and boos greeted this remark coupled with cries of ' Dictator.' The objectors said that in view of this speech beforehand, the Minister was biassed and had not approached his task with an open mind. The House of Lords, however, pointed out that no judicial or quasi-judicial duty at all was imposed on the Minister and that any reference to judicial duty or bias was irrelevant. He was right to have a policy in the matter and could not be expected to come with a blank mind to it. The only question was whether he did in fact genuinely consider the inspector's report and the objections : and as there was no evidence that he had not done so, his order was good.

Before this case and other recent cases it had been commonly understood by lawyers that the inspector at the local inquiry, and the Minister in considering his order, must act, as it were, judicially, and must observe the elementary rules applicable to judicial functions, such as to allow each party to deal with information adverse to him.[20] That view must now, it appears, be regarded as wrong. The Minister in these matters is not exercising judicial

---

[20] See, for instance, *Errington* v. *Minister of Health* [1935] 1 K.B. 249 ; and an article by H. W. R. Wade in 10 Camb.L.J. 216. The observations in *Rice's Case* [1911] A.C. at p. 182, and *Arlidge's Case* [1915] A.C. at p. 132, must be taken to relate to judicial functions.

functions, but administrative functions. The safeguards against abuse of his powers are not to be found
by requiring him to act judicially but requiring him to
follow the prescribed code of procedure, that is to say,
a ' local inquiry ' at which objectors can be heard, an
inspector's report, and consideration by the Minister
of the report. So long as the statutory procedure is
complied with and the Minister genuinely considers
the matter, the courts will not interfere.

It would be a mistake, however, to suppose that,
as a result of the Stevenage case, the courts are left
with no control over the abuse of power. The House
of Lords said significantly that the powers must be
' genuinely ' exercised. This requirement of genuine-
ness brings us back to the principle of ' détournement
de pouvoir '. In order that a power should be
genuinely exercised, the administrator must have the
proper state of mind—the state of mind which
Parliament expects him to have—the state of mind
of an administrator who carefully investigates all the
relevant considerations and rejects all irrelevant ones ;
who will fairly balance public interest and private
right : and thereupon after due consideration come
to an honest decision as to whether to exercise the
power, or not, for the purpose authorised by
Parliament. If the courts are satisfied that he did
not bring that state of mind to bear on the matter—or
that his action was so unreasonable that he cannot
have brought it to bear—then the courts will interfere.
If this principle is vigorously applied by the courts,
we may yet find in the courts protection against undue
encroachment on our liberties by the executive.

NON-USE OF POWER

So far I have dealt with the misuse of power by its wrongful exercise. But what is to happen when a public authority does not exercise a power which it ought to exercise ? Suppose that a public authority which has power to issue licences delays consideration of applications indefinitely, has the party injured any remedy ? It might easily happen for instance that the roof of a man's house leaked and he needed a licence to do the repairs, but the local authority put off consideration of it indefinitely whilst the water soaked his goods. Or a business man might have an urgent call abroad and the Treasury might defer consideration of his application for the necessary currency until the business was lost. In France they have a general principle which covers such cases. The administrative courts have laid it down that the executive are under a general duty to exercise due diligence. The courts there will not tolerate inertia or procrastination. The public authorities cannot simply do nothing and escape responsibility. So the Commune de Roquecourbe, which had power to control the use of a dangerous shooting range, was declared responsible because the Mayor had not taken steps either to prohibit its use or to make it safe, as a result of which an accident occurred.[21]

There is, so far as I know, as yet no corresponding principle in English law. In early days the common law often held that a power was coupled with a duty. If a thief stole goods and a constable had reasonable

[21] Anglo-French Legal Conference, 1947, p. 88.

grounds for knowing who was the culprit, he not only had a power to arrest, but he also was under a duty to arrest him. If a highway authority which had power to repair a highway did not repair it so that it became founderous, they were indictable for a nuisance. The civil remedies for a breach of the duty to repair are most inadequate, but the duty certainly existed.

Any hope of developing any duty of diligence comparable with that imposed by the French administrative law has however received a check by a recent decision of the House of Lords. A farmer in Suffolk, whose land was near a tidal river, was flooded out when the high tides broke the walls which protected his land. The Catchment Board had power to mend the banks and they started to do so. But they went about it very badly. They tried to drive a dam straight across the bank and the materials were washed away by the tides : whereas they ought to have built out a semi-circular dam so as to exclude the tides from the breach whilst they repaired the gap. The result of this inefficiency was that it was six months before the bank was made good, instead of only two weeks : and the farmer suffered great loss because of course his land remained flooded. Nevertheless the House of Lords held that he had no remedy. Their reason was that the Catchment Board had a power to do the work, but were under no duty to do it. If they had done nothing, they would not have been liable : so why should they be liable because they took a long time over it ? Lord Atkin strongly dissented. He declared that the Catchment

Board were under a duty to act with reasonable diligence, that is, with reasonable despatch : and he added ' I cannot imagine this House affording its support to a proposition so opposed to public interests when there are so many public bodies exercising statutory powers and employing public money upon them.' Yet the House did afford its support to the proposition.[22]

Whether there is any possibility of distinguishing that case, hereafter, I do not know : but at any rate it only applies where it is clear that the power is not coupled with a duty. There are many powers which are by necessary intendment coupled with a duty : and when that is so the High Court will always intervene to see that the duty is performed. An example occurred recently when a widow made a claim for a pension on account of the death of her husband who died from an obscure disease. The claim was put on one side by the Ministry—from their point of view quite reasonably—to await the decision of a test case about this disease. But they did it without her consent. She did not see why her claim should be held up, and asked for a mandamus to compel the Ministry to deal with it. And it was dealt with.

CONCLUSION

This brings me to the end of these lectures. Reviewing the position generally, the chief point which emerges is that we have not yet settled the principles upon which to control the new powers of

[22] *East Suffolk Catchment Board* v. *Kent* [1941] A.C. 74.

the executive. No one can suppose that the executive will never be guilty of the sins that are common to all of us. You may be sure that they will sometimes do things which they ought not to do : and will not do things that they ought to do. But if and when wrongs are thereby suffered by any of us, what is the remedy ? Our procedure for securing our personal freedom is efficient, but our procedure for preventing the abuse of power is not. Just as the pick and shovel is no longer suitable for the winning of coal, so also the procedure of mandamus, certiorari, and actions on the case are not suitable for the winning of freedom in the new age. They must be replaced by new and up to date machinery, by declarations, injunctions, and actions for negligence[23] : and, in judicial matters, by compulsory powers to order a case stated. This is not a task for Parliament. Our representatives there cannot control the day to day activities of the many who administer the manifold activities of the State : nor can they award damages to those who are injured by any abuses. The courts must do this. Of all the great tasks that lie ahead, this is the greatest. Properly exercised the new powers of the executive lead to the Welfare State : but abused they lead to the totalitarian State. None such must ever be allowed in this country. We have in our time to deal with changes which are of equal constitutional significance to those which took place 300 years ago. Let us prove ourselves equal to the challenge.

[23] See an article on ' The Courts and the Administrative Process ' by Prof. E. C. S. Wade, 63 L.Q.R. 164.